ST. PAUL'S CHURCH AND SCHOOL
PARISH OF NEWBARNS AND HAWCOAT
BARROW IN FURNESS

THE STORY RECORDED IN
CHURCH MAGAZINES AND SCHOOL LOG BOOKS

St. Paul's Church and School
Parish of
Newbarns and Hawcoat
Barrow in Furness
1843 - 1993

© Sidney Bundy
ISBN 0 9520641 0 3   The History of St. Paul's Church & School

ACKNOWLEDGEMENTS

I wish to express my gratitude to:-

Mary Jenkin	-for editing the articles in the Parish Post which led to the production of this book.
My wife, Phyllis	-for patiently typing all my manuscripts.
Geoff Parkes	-for his willingness to respond to my requests in producing the cover design and numerous sketches from old prints and items of church furniture.
Marion Muddiman	-(who was a pupil at St. Paul's during my period as Headmaster) for expert work on the word processor and her positive assurance that this book was possible.
John Winder	-(pupil at St. Paul's during Miss G. Fallows period as Headmistress) for his interest and keeness that a book should be produced for the 150th Anniversary and especially for the use of facilities in his office.
Blitz Pictures	-Courtesy of the Barrow Museum
Acknowledge	-The Kirby Archive Trust for encouragement and financial support
Dominic Ruscillo	-(of Guardian Inprint Limited) for his help and advice most willingly given.

Sidney P. Bundy
Headmaster 1947 - 70
Vice Chairman P.C.C. 1973 - 93
Deputy Church Warden 1985 - 93

CONTENTS

Foreword

FOREWORD

By the Revd. Christopher Jenkin,
Team Rector

It is important for a church to know its history. We need to understand our roots; the present congregation of a church has not sprung, out of the blue, into existence! Its traditions, its strengths and weaknesses, and the way it is regarded by members of the local community, are all profoundly affected by the past.

There are two dangers, equal and opposite. One is to say, with Henry Ford, "History is bunk!", and to behave as if we were starting with a clean slate. But the other is to live in the past, and to regard it with a fond nostalgia, ignoring the fact that time has moved on.

When I was at college, the man who taught us Church History always started with a prayer: "Lord, help us so to understand the past that we may live for thee today."

As we read this fascinating history of our Church, St. Paul's, may that be the prayer of every present member of the church family, both those who can remember many of the events recounted, and the people mentioned for many years past, and those new arrivals to whom it might just be "ancient history".

We are grateful indeed to Sid Bundy, who is surely well qualified to undertake this task, that he has produced this "labour of love" for all of us.

ST. PAUL'S CHURCH AND SCHOOL
PARISH OF NEWBARNS AND HAWCOAT
BARROW IN FURNESS

School

ST. PAUL'S
C of E
SCHOOL

1843 - 1993

St. Paul's

Parish of Newbarns & Hawcoat

Church

1871 - 199

THE STORY RECORDED IN
CHURCH MAGAZINES AND SCHOOL LOG BOOKS

CHAPTER 1
Introduction

In 1970, to commemorate the 100th Anniversary of the building of St. Paul's Church, Horace Hayhurst, Churchwarden, undertook the formidable but rewarding task of writing a history of St. Paul's Church and School.

Mr. H. Hayhurst Church Warden 1958-1978

The completion of this task coincided with the dedication of the extension of the church which had been envisaged for many years. Prior to 1970, St. Paul's Church looked incomplete. The church entrance was a disgrace. The job of welcoming people to church in such a congested area was almost impossible.

Now twenty years on, it seems appropriate to examine the contents of Horace's book to give the many 'new' families, and those who have grown-up from the 'old' families, the opportunity to look back at the past and forward into the future.

As we move into the Decade of Evangelism, new ideas may be needed so that our church building may be able to fulfil the needs of the present time. For the past five years, during the ministries of the Revd. Frank Dean and the Revd. Christopher Jenkin, the need for space at the entrance or at the side of the building has been under discussion. Plans are already in hand to improve toilet and kitchen arrangements. More ambitious plans have been closely examined and are at present 'on hold', perhaps to be re-examined during the next ten years.

With these thoughts in mind, it is hoped to publish in the Parish Post a series of articles based on Horace's book and brought-up-to-date to mark the 120th Anniversary of the building of St. Paul's Church.

Barrow in 1843

Horace Hayhurst introduced the story of St. Paul's Church and School by referring to the population figures in 1806 when Barrow Village numbered 65, Newbarns 40 and Hawcoat 71. By 1843 the population of Barrow Village had risen to an estimated figure of 150 in 28 houses - I do not have the figures for Newbarns and Hawcoat. Lancashire and Furness formed part of the Diocese of Chester, and it was not until 1856 that these districts of North West Lancashire were transferred to the Diocese of Carlisle. Barrow and the surrounding villages were all within the ancient parish of Dalton.

The School and the Chapel of Ease

In the Foreword to the book, the Revd. Frank Dean, newly appointed Vicar of St. Paul's, stated "Big Trees from Little Acorns Grow." It is a long trail from the little schoolroom church of 1843 to the attractive church that is St. Paul's today, so I feel it is very necessary to quote from the book to illustrate this point:-

For some time before 1843, the Bishop of Chester, the Right Rev. J.B. Summer, D.D., and the Vicar of Dalton, the Rev. J.T. Kirkbank, M.A., had given earnest consideration to the necessity of satisfying the spiritual needs of the people of Barrow and the surrounding villages. The difficulty was finding a minister to take the duty. Finally a piece of land situated in Barrow Lane, now Abbey Road at the corner of the present Ilkley Road, "being part of a field known as Stackhouse Rysal in the Division of Newbarns and within the Manor of Plain Furness containing one rood and one perch statute measure was staked and mered out" and on October 17th, 1842, was conveyed by Mr. Edward Lesh, Yeoman, and Jane, his wife of Newbarns to Mr. T.Y.P. Michaelson of the Isle of Barrow in consideration of the sum of nineteen guineas.

On May 28th, 1843, a meeting was held in Barrow when "the landowners and inhabitants of the villages of Newbarns, Hawcoat, Salthouse and Barrow and of the farms and places adjoining, all in the parish of Dalton, being desirous of having a schoolhouse erected within some part of the said district for the purpose of educating therein the children of the neighbour-hood, and wherein also the public worship according to the rites of the Established Church of England might be performed", unanimously decided to build a school. A committee was formed for carrying out the project and to solicit subscriptions in aid of the building. Mr. T.Y.P. Michaelson then conveyed the premises he had bought by means of a Trust Deed dated September 28th, 1843, to James T. Kirkbank, M.A., of Dalton, the Rev. T. Marshall Postlethwaite, B.A., of Millwood, the Rev. John Baldwin, M.A. of Dalton and John Cranke, gentleman of Hindpool, all of whom, including Mr. Michaelson were named as Trustees.

The school, 50 feet long and 23 feet wide, was built of local sandstone from Hawcoat Quarry by Richard Briggs and William Barban, stone-masons of Dalton, and Edward Deason, joiner of Newton, and walled off from the remaining part of the field. Part of the wall, topped with limestone coping still stands in Ilkley Road as part of the boundary wall of No. 253 Abbey Road, a silent tribute to the lasting qualities of local stone. Additions were made in 1856-60 of a porch and new bell turret, and a schoolmaster's house was added in 1886 adjoining the western gable.

On November 4th, 1843, the Bishop of Chester licensed the new building as follows:

"To all whom it may concern:

Whereas the inhabitants of Barrow, in the Parish of Dalton-in-Furness are so far distant from the parish church that many of them are unable to attend the same; and whereas a schoolroom has been erected in that hamlet capable of being conveniently used for the purpose of divine worship: Be it hereby known that the Rev. J.T. Kirkbank, Vicar of Dalton, has our license to use the said schoolroom for public service according to the Liturgy of the United Churches of England and Ireland, and the inhabitants of the parish to attend the same.

Palace, Chester, November 4th, 1843.

J.B. Chester"

The Rev. John Baldwin, of Dalton, volunteered his professional services at the chapel, which services he performed without fees or reward for a period of eleven years. The Duke of Buccleuch gave £5 per annum to cover the expenses incurred in making these weekly journeys between Dalton and Newbarns.

The first service was held on Sexagesima, Sunday February 11th, 1844, and on every Sunday afternoon following."

From the Diary of William Fisher,

Yeoman Farmer, Barrow 1811 - 1859.

"1844 February

The new Chapel at three lanes end Barrow was opened by the Reverend John Boldwin (Baldwin) Dalton. The congregation was so large that many were obliged to stand at the outside"

Hayhurst's books continues:-

"The service was simple in form, there being no instrumental music, but an adult choir led the hymns and psalms, these being printed on

3

sheets of paper and no hymn books used.

The first schoolmaster, William Jackson, who had only one arm, rang the bell, acted as clerk and leader of the choir and sounded the key note on a pitch pipe. James Picthall, shoemaker of Gleaston, regarded as a competent musician came once a week to train the choir.

In 1853, the congregation presented a Bagster's Comprehensive Bible to the Rev. John Baldwin "not as a reward for services long and faithfully rendered, but as a mark of their esteem and respect". After his death in 1855, the services were conducted by the Rev. J.M. Morgan, Vicar of Dalton or by one of his curates up to the year 1869, and from thence by the Rev. Thomas Goss, who became the first vicar of St,. Paul's. The last service in the school was held on Sunday July 23rd, 1871.

In 1874 a portion of the school ground was acquired by the Barrow Corporation for the purpose of widening Abbey Road, and in 1877 the building itself was pulled down and a new school built on a site in Hawcoat Lane, by the Barrow Corporation in exchange for the old site in Abbey Road. The sandstone from the old building was used in the erection of the new one. The old school bell was removed and re-hung in the new belfry. The new building originally consisted of a large room later divided into two classrooms, a bell room used as an infants classroom and later as a store, and two small porches. The school was opened on September 26th, 1879. Extensive additions were made in 1887 when the main room and two more porches were built.

THE ORIGINAL ST PAUL'S SCHOOL IN 1843

The bell room was divided by a partition in 1949 to provide an office for the headmaster. A sliding partition was erected in the main room in 1913. It was removed in 1961.

During the air raids of 1941 the building suffered structural damage and was unfit for use. Lessons were carried on in the church for a fortnight and then in the Furness Cricket Pavilion for another month, by which time repairs had been effected, and the scholars moved back to the school. It continued to serve as St. Paul's School until 1957 when the first phase of the new school was finished and declared open by Mrs. W.D. Opher on 19th October. Classes were still held in it until it was finally taken over as a church hall when the new school was completed and officially opened by Viscount Knollys on September 30th, 1960.

Considerable alterations were made to the building in 1961. The boiler had been converted from solid fuel to oil firing in 1960. The outside conveniences and dividing wall were demolished, and the porch and cloak room at the south end were converted into a kitchen. The stage platform erected a few years previously was moved from the south to the north end of the main hall and a proscenium added. The centre sliding partition was removed and a new ceiling fixed and fluorescent lighting installed. The belfry was taken down and one of the original porches converted into a toilet. The total cost of these alterations was over £1,500. Since then extra repairs to the interior wall, new main windows and repairs to the roof have cost a further £1,200."

St Paul's National School 1877

A RECORD OF THE
NEWBARNS AND HAWCOAT DAY SCHOOL
Now called
ST. PAUL'S JUNIOR AND INFANTS' SCHOOL

This was the title of an article written by my predecessor, Miss Gertrude Fallows, and unearthed by Mary Jenkin, Editor of Parish Post, in the September 1941 issue of the Parish Magazine. It contains much that is known, but some paragraphs are worth quoting. The pupils of the school in 1879 were drawn from the two small villages and farms of Hawcoat and Old Newbarns - hence the original name. This was probably altered in 1933 when "all age" elementary schools became Junior and Infant Schools, and the children of eleven years and over were transferred to Central Schools, later to be called Secondary Modern Schools.

I quote only from two or three paragraphs which serve to supplement what I have already written about the Old School.

"The building when opened on September 26th 1879 consisted of the present infant room and the next room divided by a curtain, together with the bell room and two small porches. As yet, there was no large room with slide as we have at the present time. The roll of the school consisted of 66 children - 28 boys and 38 girls. In 1883 Miss Boulton, the first head-teacher, resigned and was succeeded by Miss Maria Scott, who later in the same year was followed by Miss Ella Kay, who in 1884 was replaced by Miss Ellenthorpe.

In this year an alteration to the school building was made and the one room previously divided by a curtain was converted into two classrooms. When Miss Ellenthorpe resigned in 1885 the first headmaster, Mr. Catterall, was appointed. He was succeeded in 1887 by Mr. Weatherby, whose term of office lasted only from January to May of that year, and he was followed by Mr. Algernon Pike who remained only until June. Mr. Helm, the father of Miss Marjorie Helm, a member of the present staff, was appointed to the headship, and remained in office until 1917."

HEADTEACHERS OF ST. PAUL'S SCHOOL

(Extract from School Log Book)

26. 9.1879 - 15. 6.1883	Julia C. Boulton	3 yrs 9 mnths
18. 6.1883 - 25. 8.1883	Maria Jane Scott	2 mnths 1 wk
27. 8.1883 - 19. 4.1884	Ellen Kay	7 mnths 3 wks
23. 4.1884 - 16. 7.1885	Annie Ellenthorpe	1 year 3 mnths
10. 8.1885 - 14. 1.1887	Mr. W.H. Catterall	1 year 5 mnths
17. 1.1887 - 20. 4.1888	Mr. Weatherby	1 year 3 mnths
7. 5.1888 - 1. 6.1888	Mr. Algernon Pike	1 month
1. 6.1888 - 27. 7.1917	Mr. Albert Joseph Helm	29 yrs 2 mnths
28. 8.1917 - 30. 9.1931	Mrs. Bessie Cooke	14 years 1 mnth
1.10.1931 - 31.10.1947	Miss Gertrude Fallows	16 years 1 mnth
1.11.1947 - 31. 8.1970	Mr. Sidney P. Bundy	23 years
1. 9.1970 - 31. 8.1989	Mr. Hilary J. Riley	19 years
1. 9.1989 -	Mr. Richard R.W. Sanderson	

CHAPTER 2

St. Paul's Church 1871 - 1991

In his chapter headed "St. Paul's Church", Horace Hayhurst gave details of the expansion of trade with the coming of the railway, the building of the steelworks in Hindpool and the important founding of the shipbuilding industry. This expansion was accompanied naturally by a great increase in the population figures. Barrovians numbered 3135 in 1861 and 18,911 in the next census of 1871. The town grew rapidly in these years.

"Houses had appeared along Abbey road at East and West Mount, Spring Bank and Alexandra Terrace. The Strawberry Gardens Hotel had been built in 1870. The country outside the town still retained its rural appearance apart from isolated houses at West View, Risedale Villa and Fairfield. Hawcoat Village and Newbarns remained practically unchanged and were approached from Abbey Road by narrow winding lanes, Hawcoat Lane and Hollow Lane. The junction of these two lanes with Abbey Road was known locally as Four Lane Ends.

This was the scene in 1870 when a decision to build a church was made. The Ecclesiastical District of Newbarns and Hawcoat had been formed out of the Parish of Dalton by an Order in Council of Her Majesty Queen Victoria on 7th August, 1869.

A meeting of inhabitants and friends was held in the Newbarns Schoolroom on 1st April 1870, the Reverend Thomas Goss, who had been appointed to serve the new district, acting as Chairman. The meeting was unanimous in its decision to build a new church, and a committee was formed to canvas the district. Mr. William Lesh offered to present a site at Four Lane Ends being part of a field known as Wheatclose, and the offer was gratefully accepted. Plans and estimates were obtained, and the committee accepted the design submitted by Messrs. Habershon and Brock of London. The contract to build the first portion of the complete church, which included the sanctuary, chancel and part of the nave enclosed by a temporary west wall, was placed with Mr. James Garden, of Dalton and Barrow, the estimate being £1,630 inclusive of all charges. The final cost with furnishings amounted to about £2,000.

The Diocesan Church Extension Society made a grant of £223 on certain specified conditions, the chief being that the pews should be spaced at not less than two feet ten inches apart.

The offer by the Barrow Corporation to erect boundary walls and suitable gates along Abbey Road and Hawcoat Lane in return for permission to widen these roads was accepted.

It was unanimously agreed to dedicate the church to St. Paul."

So a period of twenty eight years had elapsed from the building of the school-chapel to the erection of the present building on the corner of Hawcoat Lane and Abbey Road.

The new church was dedicated on 27th July, 1871, by the Lord Bishop of Carlisle, Dr. Harvey Goodwin, and the Reverend J.L. Morgan, M.A., of Dalton acting as Bishop's Chaplain. Amongst those present were the Mayor, James Ramsden (later Sir James) and his family.

In his address the Bishop "rejoiced in being permitted to dedicate to the service of God this first portion of the church of St. Paul". He trusted it would not be long before the temporary west wall was knocked down and the church finished. The Vicar, the Revd. Thomas Goss, who had conducted the services in the old school-chapel since 1869, named Mr. W. Lesh as his warden and Mr. W. Waite was elected as people's warden.

VICARS OF THIS PARISH

1870 - 1880	Thomas Goss, MA.
1880 - 1884	Charles Elrington-Bisset, MA.
1884 - 1893	John Henderson
1893 - 1896	James Muller, MA.
1896 - 1920	William Berry, MA.
1920 - 1940	William Taylor
1940 - 1948	Norman Robinson, BSc.
1948 - 1953	J. Arthur Briggs, MA., BD.
1953 - 1959	E.J. Hay Hicks, ALCD.
1959 - 1970	A.R. Fountain, MA.
1970 - 1987	F.A. Dean, BD, ALCD.
1988 -	Christopher Jenkin, MA

Completion of St. Paul's Church

or

The Church Extension

When the church was dedicated on 27th July 1871, the Lord Bishop of Carlisle in his address "rejoiced" in being permitted to dedicate to the service of God this first portion of the Church of St. Paul". He trusted that it would not be long before the temporary west wall was knocked down and the church was finished. As we might say today, "Famous last words!" because as we know this event did not take place until almost a century later. The Bishop's words went unheeded but during the succeeding one hundred years a number of attempts were made to start the project of either fund-raising or planning for the church extension. Quoting again from Horace Hayhurst's book we read the following paragraph:-

> *"The Rev. Thomas Goss ended his ministry at St. Paul's in 1880. In the first number of the parish magazine of January 1877, he had written with reference to the church 'We all know that it is an unfinished one.' Acting under the advice of influential friends, the committee who first undertook steps to provide the much-needed church consented, instead of building a complete church, to build the half of a large one, so that if in the course of time, further accommodation should be required, it might be provided by the completion of the design. The need of enlargement has long enough been felt, the completion of the design has not yet been undertaken. Let us have patience. We all know how much easier it is to plan than to build'."*

Seventeen years were to pass, then after the induction of the Revd. James Theophilus Muller, M.A., the first venture towards church completion was made in 1896. Ambitious plans were prepared by Messrs. Paley, Austin and Paley, Ecclesiastical Architects of Lancaster. Most of the correspondence with the architect was carried out by the vicar and when he left in 1896 negotiations were suspended.

The Revd. William Berry, M.A. began his ministry in the same year and remained at St. Paul's for twenty four years. He called a meeting of parishioners in 1897, (The Parochial Church Council did not come into being until 1913) when it was decided to reconsider the matter of church extension and a working party was appointed.

> *The previous project was evidently considered to be rather ambitious and a modified scheme was submitted by the architects, embracing the extension of the nave and south aisle, new vestries and a tall bell fleche or spire in place of the tower at an estimated cost of £3,000, the building to hold four hundred and forty.*

Plans were exhibited in the church porch and an illustration of the completed church was depicted in a pamphlet circulated with the Parish Magazine in September 1897. These plans had been approved at a meeting of parishioners, but the committee were anxious to ascertain what pecuniary support they could rely upon. The response in promised donations amounted to over £700.

This attempt to complete the church was never realised and was finally relinquished through lack of support, but the intention was not forgotten.

ORIGINAL DESIGN FOR THE CHURCH EXTENSION

The advent of a new vicar, Revd. William Taylor in 1920, revived the subject again and although the parishioners, and we hope, the P.C.C. pledged themselves to raise the necessary funds, within a year, at a subsequent meeting, it was resolved that the scheme for the completion of the church be postponed for the present and priority be given to the more urgent matter of placing the income of the benefice upon a satisfactory and permanent basis. This meeting pledged itself to raise a sum of not less than £2,000 for this purpose. So fifty years on (1871-1921) the temporary west wall still remained. (It is interesting to record that a similar west wall at St. Mary's Walney, was also defying the winds from the Irish Sea until, I believe, 1928). For many years during the depression of the 1920's and 1930's and the Second World War, the plans for church completion remained 'on the statute book' although the fund for that purpose was still in existence and growing slowly. Many members of our church will be able to recall the efforts made in the 1950's and 1960's towards other pressing programmes - the building of a daughter church, St. Aidan's on the new Newbarns housing estate; the building of the Vicarage to replace the one damaged by enemy bombing in the 1940's; the building of the new St. Paul's Junior School. Finally in 1961 the P.C.C. decided to examine the merits of two schemes for church extension.

It was then decided to ask Messrs. Hargreaves and Mawson, Architects of Kendal, to prepare plans for the extension of the church, to give provision for extra seating for one hundred and fifty, and to include a suitable entrance porch. The new plans for the extension were favourably received at a Parochial Church Council meeting held on 19th March, 1962, at which the architect was present, and the design was given general approval. The church completion appeal was finally launched on Ash Wednesday, 1963, for an estimated £25,000 with the completion fund standing at £3,230. Regular and systematic giving was encouraged by the initiation of an envelope and covenant scheme. By the end of 1965 the church completion fund had reached the £10,000 mark and was growing steadily. An interest free loan of £3,000 was made from the diocese.

The contract documents with the amended plans for the extension were duly signed at a special Parochial Church Council meeting held in the vestry at 11.30 a.m. on the 20th May 1966, after a short service in the church. The contract price was £21,889 exclusive of professional fees, and subject to adjustment.

The actual building work began on the 7th June, 1966, and was favoured throughout by fair weather. A temporary entrance was made in the west wall of the south transept, and by January 1967, a hugh plastic screen had been erected to seal off the demolished west wall, thus enabling the church to be used for normal services throughout the whole building period.

The dedication ceremony took place on Friday, 15th September 1967, in the presence of a capacity congregation which included the Mayor and Mayoress and their deputies. In an impressive service of thanksgiving, the new west end was duly dedicated by the Lord Bishop of Carlisle, the Right Reverend S. Cyril Bulley, M.A. A fanfare of trumpets sounded after the prayers of dedication, and in his address, the Bishop commended the parish on its achievement, and those responsible for the building work, for their skill and craftsmanship. The main building contractor was Messrs. Chas. McWilliams (Barrow) Limited. The joinery and woodwork was carried out by Gilbert Caine Limited of Dalton and the painting and plumbing by Messrs. T. Ward and Son of Barrow. The oil-fired central heating was installed by the Strand Engineering Company and the electric wiring and public address system by Messrs. Hartley and Bramhall Limited of Barrow.

Two pews were removed from the front of the nave on each side, the font re-sited at the east end of the north transect, and the side aisles relaid with "granwood" tiling to match the floor in the extension. New carpet was laid in the nave and a floor covering fitted underneath the pews in the old portion of the church, the latter being the gift of a parishioner.

The total cost of completion was about £29,500 and this figure had not yet been reached, though the fund was growing steadily towards this end. In May 1969, a Festival of Flowers, augmented by organ and choir recitals was held. This attractive event realised a further £370 towards the completion cost. The fund was closed in June 1970 when its purpose had been achieved.

And so it came about that the image of a completed church which had constantly been in the thoughts of the people of St. Paul's ever since the church was first built, finally reached its fulfilment in time for the centenary celebrations of 1971.

This was the conclusion in 1970 when the Revd. A.R. Fountain left the parish. By the late 1980's, during the ministry of the Revd. Frank Dean, the Parochial Church Council spent many hours discussing the question of church expansion rather than extension. It was felt that space was required at the sides and/or the entrance to the church to provide the necessary freedom of movement for members to meet after services for social and informal conversation.

The Memorial Doors

The memorial doors between the foyer and the west end of the church contain etched glass panels framed in oak. They depict St. Paul and his Mediterranean journeys.

These beautiful glass doors were the gift of the Clark family in memory of Mr. William Clark (8.12.1885 - 18.6.1951) and his wife, Mrs. Emily Clark (21.7.1887 -

11.12.1966) who gave life-long service to our church. They were the parents of Mrs. Edna Postlethwaite, Mrs. Mary Jackson, Benson Clark and the late Stanley Clark.

The panels were designed and engraved by Messrs. Reed, Millican and Company of Newcastle.

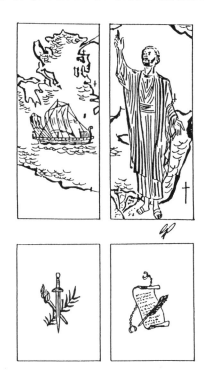

The next twenty years following our Centenary

A New Beginning. A new extension to the existing church building, and a new vicar. At the school a new headmaster following the retirement of Mr. Sid Bundy after twenty three years service. A period of our young men "going out"; Ian Honeyman taking up a choral scholarship at Kings College, Cambridge, and David Marsden and Jim Scantlebury preparing for ordination in 1971 and 1972 respectively.

1971 Centenary year opened with the "Act of Renewal", celebrated with a "Festival of Flowers", and a challenge to raise £1,000 in the "Century of Coins" (it was decimal currency year!). Clergy friends of past years and an "old boy" of the school and the choir, Revd. Alan Postlethwaite, returned to preach.

1972: Changes in our style of worship began with the introduction of the Family Service.

After celebrating fifty years as our organist and choir mistress Miss Taylor retired.

A new curate, Revd. George Thomson and his family moved into a new "curatage" in Furness Park Road.

Our CMS Link Missionaries, Geoffrey and Phyllis Gardner returned home after nineteen years in Nigeria.

1973: A new form of worship. "Series 3" Holy Communion was introduced with some difficulties, especially the simplicity of the language and the sharing of the Peace.

A new Reader, Mr. Jack Dryer and his family were welcomed into the parish. Jack had thirty six years experience of ministry to share with us in the next six years.

New CMS Link Missionaries, Drs. Bryan and Helen Thompson at St. Luke's Hospital, Hiranpur, North India, were appointed.

A new sound, "The Certain Sounds", from Van Nuys, California brought a fresh insight to praise in worship. It was a thrill to see one hundred and fifty teenagers waiting for the doors to open and to sit with over six hundred other folk to share in this vibrant sound and fresh challenge to commitment.

The Middle 70's presented a much quieter time. We welcomed a retired gentleman, Revd. Stanley Ragg, whose ministry soothed and strengthened in those memorable seven years he spent with us.

Mrs. Nancy Dawson retired after thirty years as superintendent of the Sunday School's Infant Department. Also after thirty years service, this time in the choir, Mr. Ken Hughes was transferred to Southampton. We said goodbye to Ken Bradley who had been our Reader for ten years, and his wife Margaret, leader of the Mothers' Union - they had been "re-organised". Some come, some go, and so it was with our curates; we now welcomed the Revd. David Towler and his family.

By 1977 the Church halls were completed, largely through the efforts of the Scouts to have their own building alongside.

In the months when there was a fifth Sunday, we had only one service, "God's Family Together", and so the creche facilities were introduced.

The 1970's closed with Mr. Horace Hayhurst resigning as People's Warden after twenty years; he was honoured with "Emeritus" status. He, amongst many others of his services to St. Paul's, was the author of the Church's History, its first one-hundred years.

With the passing of Miss Robson, tribute was paid to the work she and Miss Sibson had done for the PCC, the Children's Society, Christian Aid, and in keeping the Church Hall Car Park free from broken glass. Together they had totalled over eighty years service.

When is a "Young Wife" not a "Young Wife"? Mrs. Audrey Woodall decided it was after twenty eight years, fifteen of them as leader!

On Sunday, 1st July 1979, the Bishop of Manchester, the Rt. Revd. Stanley Booth-Clibborn, preached at a special service at St. Paul's, to mark the end of Barrow Grammar School for Boys and its incorporation into the comprehensive system.

The then Bishop of Sheffield, the late Rt. Revd. Gordon Fallows, a Barrovian and former pupil at the school, should have been the preacher, but was unable to attend through illness, so the Bishop of Manchester deputised for him.

1980 heralded "Journey with Jesus", the first of the Revd. Frank Dean's attempts to evangelise within the parish, this time with the help of theological students from St. John's College, Durham.

After twenty five years as CMS and SAMS Missionary Secretary, Mrs. Blanche Scarlin handed over her expertise to Mrs. Christine Maxfield. Also at this time, our

SAMS Link Missionary, Miss Barbara Kitchin, returned home to care for her Mother. She had been in South America for twenty years.

In the early 80's the ladies came more to the fore. Miss Janet Parke was studying at Capernwray Bible College before setting off for service with the Africa Evangelical Fellowship.

Mrs. Kathleen Henshaw and Mrs. Barbara Busby started the "Rendezvous", a group for Mums, Tinies and Toddlers. Miss Kath Horton was licensed as a Parochial Reader, and Miss Carol Farrer joined us as Deaconess, or "Lady Curate", as our Vicar liked to call her.

Ladies and girls joined the men and boys in the choir and on special occasions extra members of the congregation swelled their numbers.

Recognition for long and distinguished service was afforded to the leaders of our uniformed organisation; Mrs. Kath Davison, fifteen years our Brown Owl, and Mrs. Lynda Garforth, eighteen years Guide Captain; and silver Acorns were presented to Mr. Denis Stanswood, Mr. Eric Lewin and Mr. Sid Bundy by the Scout Movement.

1984 Team Ministry. With the appointment of Revd. Alan Crossley as Chaplain to the new Hospital and Team Vicar at St. Paul's, the Vicar became the Team Rector, together working with Deaconess Carol. Church members also became involved at the hospital, assisting Alan in liaising with the ward staff and escorting patients to the Chapel on Sunday mornings.

"Mission England", another call to make people aware of the work of the church, was followed up the next year with "Mission Encore".

1985: Stewards. Amidst heart searching, with the congregation at 11.00 a.m. dwindling, the 9.00 a.m. Family Communion was discontinued, the two services were replaced by the 10.00 a.m. service which would vary in its style.

The first Stewardship Campaign was run, and was followed up four years later. Service and Solvency was encouraging, the latter so necessary with the organ costing us another £5,600.

The 1980's closed with the sudden death of the Revd. Frank Dean in his seventeenth year of ministry at St. Paul's. His ardent desire to mount yet another mission, "Come Alive", went ahead as scheduled, and was led by Mr. Derek Simpson in the Autumn of 1987.

Mary and Norman Davies left the parish after Norman's retirement. They had served as Superintendents in the Sunday School, and Norman had also been a Reader and latterly had been Church Warden.

St. Paul's Scout Troup celebrated seventy years, and along with the world-wide Movement opened a group for younger boys, the "Beavers".

Rev. Frank Dean 1970-1987
Baptism of Caroline Jane Barker, daughter
of Graham and Jane Barker, and
great-granddaughter of Phyllis & Sid Bundy

Rev. Christopher Jenkin
1988 -

The Church Fellowship celebrated its fifty years, most of those with Mr. Bill Parke at its helm. Mrs. Gertrude James, for many years a member of St. Paul's celebrated her 100th Birthday.

Our new Rector, the Revd. Chris Jenkin, arrived with his family and threw himself fully into his new job, and into the immediate task of raising £4,000 for the Church Urban Fund. Remarkably, by the imaginative and enthusiastic leadership of Mr. Sid Bundy, this target was well passed within three months.

There were changes at the school, where Headmaster, Mr. Hilary Riley (19 years), and Deputy Head, Mrs. Williams (34 years) took their well-earned retirements.

A very expensive overhaul to the organ was undertaken, and an even more expensive one awaits.

The 1990's and the Decade of Evangelism. Teams of lay folk have been taking monthly services in three of the Retirement Homes in the Parish. "Christians In Hawcoat", an ecumenical outreach to the many homes on the estate, provided a monthly service. Revd. Stephen Wright, who had replaced Deaconess Carol, and had held the fort during the interregnum after Frank Dean's death, was himself replaced by the Revd. Steve Osman, with Jean and all the little Osmans.

The death occurred of retired Prebendary Malcolm McNicol, who with his wife Elizabeth had joined us in 1981, and in 1987 had celebrated his fifty years in the Ministry.

Older Sunday School children, the Explorers and the Pathfinders, started to meet in church for the first part of the service before going on to their sessions. Healing

Ministry was made available within the Holy Communion services at 10.00 a.m. and 6.30 p.m.

Not to be outdone by the Beavers in Scouting, we welcomed the Rainbows to the Guide Association.

During these twenty years we supported the Bishop's "Harvest for the Hungry" appeals, and also appeals for Sudan, Poland and Rumania; we regularly assisted Christian Aid, Leprosy Mission, CMB, SAMS, C. of E. Children's Society and the British and Foreign Bible Society.

As a parish we have enjoyed weekends at Thornleigh (Grange), Blaithwaite (near Wigton), and Scargill (Yorkshire Dales). Together we have gone on rambles, been to Rydal Hall, attended open air services at the Park and in Furness Abbey, and enjoyed annual visits to the Keswick Convention, and more recently to Prom Praise.

Our young people have also enjoyed their weekends and summer camps with Pathfinders, Scripture Union and CYFA. The Choir have had their away training days too. Scouts and Guides have always enjoyed their many camps, none more than the joint venture to Germany.

Rendezvous, CYFA, Mothers' Union and the fellowship all continue to serve one another in social activities in a Christian atmosphere. Together we have had much fun with Sponsored Knits and Sings, Fireworks, Bonfires and Barbecues, Open Days, Picnics, Suppers, Parties, Musical Events, and many "Welcomes" and "Farewells". Our Bible Study and Lent Groups, Confirmation Classes and Saints Alive groups have all helped, along with the magazine ministry, to bring us together in friendship, fellowship and with a common aim, to proclaim that "Jesus is Lord".

In all this joy and busyness we have not lost sight of or reverence for our Holy and Almighty God and Father, and we can thank God for our greater understanding of Him and of each other.

> C.Y.F.A. - Stands for Church Youth Fellowship Association
> PROH PRAISE - was a service of Praise and Worship Services
> in different churches throughout the diocese
> ***************

Miss Kathleen Horton spent many hours reading past issues of the Parish Magazine to put together this comprehensive review of the twenty years following our Centenary. It is good to record changes in the membership of our church, and the endeavours to improve our aims as a caring, evangelistic church. Many other parishioners, too numerous to mention, have contributed to these changes, and we remember them with thankfulness.

The Church Foyer
Alterations and Renovations - 1992

In 1971 the Parish rejoiced. The Church Completion was a fact, or so we thought. By the mid 80's during the Ministry of the Rev. Frank Dean it was obvious that more had to be done. There was apparently no 'finality' where Church Completion was concerned. The problem arose when it was decided to provide tea, coffee or orange juice after the morning service, thus giving the congregation the opportunity to mix, discuss the 'sermon' and get to know each other. At St. Paul's we know many faces, a number of names, but fewer combinations of names and faces! This was a wonderful idea but space was limited unless we had an overflow from the foyer into the church.

All we could do was to put tables and chairs into the ambulatory and to remove the coat racks to provide space for the serving of the refreshments.

Many churches have been faced with the same situation. We in the Anglican Church have lagged behind the Non-Conformist churches who planned access from the Church into the Church Rooms when the buildings were designed. In the "Abbey Road churches" this can be seen in the former Emmanuel Church, the Methodist and Baptist Churches. In recent years, some churches have overcome this lack of space by converting part of the church building into Parish Rooms. This can be seen at St. George's and St. Mark's.

To return to our problem - in 1987 the Parochial Church Council had a visitation from the Archdeacon and the situation was reviewed. We adjourned from the church into the vestry and the various ideas put forward by P.C.C. members were discussed. One idea was to build a balcony room or second storey above the extended part of the church, but the most important matter was to find a solution to the damp and frequent penetration of rain from the church entrance roof. This problem had to be the main consideration. Before any action could be taken the Rev. Frank Dean died and the matter was left in abeyance.

I have enlisted the help of Mr. Michael Ralph who has submitted this report on the events which followed the interregnum.

> "The appointment of the Revd. Christopher Jenkin in January 1988 set the wheels in motion again and a Building Sub-Committee was formed in March of that year. The brief was to consider extending the south ambulatory and alter internally the porch area. Architects Messrs. Craig and Green were asked to produce preliminary plans and estimate the approximate cost of this work. Plans were drawn up by June 1988. Variations on this theme were considered on several occasions but by January 1989, the estimated cost was getting out of all proportion, for its benefit, at about £100,000. This did include a pitched roof over the porch and side ambulatory, to get rid of the flat roof problems we have, and provide disabled access of toilet.
>
> Over the next months a lot of work was put in to try to salvage something from all the ideas, but in March 1990, the extension plans were laid to rest as the cost was too high and we could not afford the expense.
>
> Specifications were drawn up for limited internal alterations and work to stop leaks in the gable end. In September 1990 an estimate from Messrs. Gilbert and Caine was accepted for these repairs etc., and a faculty obtained from Carlisle for the work to go ahead.
>
> The alterations involve turning the little store room where at present the creche toys are kept into a kitchen, with a hatch through which tea or coffee can be served; thus removing the interior wall behind the bookstall, thus opening up the area; enlarging the store room behind the War Memorial; and turning the Gents toilet into a unisex Disabled

Toilet. In addition, a ramp will be built at the main door to allow easier access for disabled people."

From the Parish Post of March 1992 the Rector writes:

The New Entrance

On the 17th May for the first time we used the new entrance and foyer. Like all building work, it took longer than expected, and we were impatient to see it completed. But at last it was done (apart from one or two minor details which we hope will be done shortly), and we were able to come into the church the right way.

Everyone has expressed surprise at how much more space there is. After all, we had only removed an internal part-wall! But with that gone, and the new carpet making the new area one whole, it gives us a lovely sense of spaciousness.

When we served tea after the 10 o'clock service that day, it was great to be out of the poky corner, and to be able to spread ourselves. The ladies were delighted with the new pantry and serving hatch.

Though we had considered plans for much more extensive alterations, enlarging the foyer towards Hawcoat Lane, or the ambulatory towards Abbey road, the increased space achieved seemed hardly worth the very large sums involved, so we settled for the more modest scheme.

Disabled

There is now a ramp up to the main door, so that wheel-chairs can get in easily. Furthermore, to help any disabled worshippers, the Gentleman's toilet has been converted for the use of disabled people - of either sex. We hope that support bars and other aids will be fitted there shortly.

Though at present we have no regular worshippers who are disabled, we can now welcome such folk more confidently! (Maybe they haven't come before, because of the difficulty of negotiating the step, etc.).

Of course, for those who wear deaf aids, we have had for some time an Induction Loop - turn the switch on the deaf aid to "T" and you will pick up the signal direct from the microphones.

Fellowship

The purpose of all these alterations is to help the sense of fellowship - of worshippers belonging to one another in God's family. If everyone slips away from a service as soon as it is over, with no contact or conversation with other members, the "fellowship of the Holy Spirit" hasn't got a chance. That's why we serve tea and squash after the 10 o'clock service.

When it was first suggested that tea or coffee should be served some years ago, there were those who disapproved strongly - "if people are thirsty, they can go home for a drink!" But what if they are lonely or just want a chance to mix, chat casually, or share a problem? To do these things over a cuppa offers a pleasant and natural way of building relationships - and relationships are meant, in God's plan to be a central part of life in Christ's church.

CHAPTER 3

Anniversaries - Memorials - Furnishings

Anniversaries of birthdays, wedding days and other important days in one's private life are usually celebrated by the exchange of gifts. In the life of a church this has taken the form of donations of furnishings or money and in some cases, the gift of a memorial plaque to mark the life and service of a church member or prominent citizen. Over the years these donations have been recorded in issues of the Parish Magazine and the acceptance of furnishings and memorials entered into the Terrier or Inventory of church goods by the church wardens who are responsible for the safe keeping of such things. In his book, Horace Hayhurst quotes an entry in the terrier in 1894. Whether this entry concerns gifts is not stated but it shows that the church wardens of that day had an easier time when checking the inventory.

> *"The terrier, or inventory of goods belonging to the church in 1894 listed, one Flagon, one Chalice, two Patens, one Alms Dish, four Collecting Plates, one Prayer Book and one Bible, one Book of Offices, one Communion Cloth, one Fair Linen Cloth, one Surplice, one Iron Chest and one Bell. One Font and one Lectern, one Painted Window (The William Lesh memorial window in the South transect) and one Marble Tablet. The Vicar at this time was the Revd. James Theophilus Muller."*

The acceptance of these gifts, although appreciated, has to be controlled or else the churches could be "cluttered" with good intentions. This control is effected by applying for a Faculty which enables the quality and appropriateness of the gift to be assessed. The system of applying for a Faculty is explained in the "Handbook for Churchwardens and Church Councillors", - it is a kind of "ecclesiastical planning permission".

In researching the Parish Magazines of the last one hundred and twenty years, certain anniversaries have been "red letter days" marked by celebrations and gifts. The year 1921 marks the Golden Jubilee of the dedication of St. Paul's Church. In the Vicar's Letter of the February issue of the Church Magazine of 1931 he refers to this occasion in these words:-

> *"It will be remembered that the Jubilee ten years ago was marked by the very successful effort of raising a fund towards the increase of the income of the Benefice (the Vicar's salary). This was done by the unanimous decision of the Church Council. Other objects which have been achieved during the last ten years include:-*

1.The War Memorial Bronze at a cost of £75.

2.The Electric Lighting of the Church at a cost of £120.

3.The building of Motor Room housing Motor Blower and cleaning the organ at a cost of £260.

4.The renovation of the Vicarage at a cost of £164 with a grant of £111 from the Ecclesiastical Commissioners in addition.

5.The Mary Smith Memorial Window depicting the Annunciation - cost £50.

6.The marble flooring and platform in the Sanctuary.

The gifts to the church during these years, including the Reredos and Panelling, Holy Table, Kneeling Desks, the Bishop's Chair, three other Memorial Windows in the Chancel and the East Window, represent a total cost of about £1,340."

The vicar has expressed the hope that the Diamond Jubilee to be celebrated on 27th July 1931, would be worthy of the occasion. So, on Sunday 24th July 1931, the Diamond Jubilee was celebrated in St. Paul's Church. The Lord Bishop of Carlisle preached at the service of Morning Prayer at 10.30 a.m. On Thursday, 28th July a Garden Party was held at Drummard, Hawcoat Lane. The Shipyard Prize Band was in attendance. The Vicar asked friends who had motor cars if they would use them to give "Joy Rides" at a shilling a head!

On 22nd November 1931, at the 10.30 a.m. service, the Bishop of Barrow dedicated the new Pulpit, Choir Stalls, Panelling and Marble Floor.

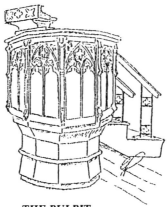

THE PULPIT

This completed the East End of the Church and was inspired by the gifts of the Holy Table and other furnishings previously mentioned. Two other items of furniture worth noting were the brass Lectern and the brass Sanctuary Rail, which was the gift of Councillor James Fisher, J.P. in 1902.

The Brass Lectern
The brass lectern is housed in the Barrow Museum.
We are indebted to the curator, Mr. David Tull, who produced coloured photographs
from which this sketch has been made.

During 1931 - 32 a subscription list was started as a memorial for Mr. J.H. Odgers, late Sunday School Superintendent and church warden. This was to take the form of a new font of Derbyshire Alabaster with a Coniston Slate base. It replaced the old sandstone font and was dedicated on 10th June, 1934.

SANDSTONE FONT

This font has now been renovated in 1992 and stands on the north side of the church near the vestry. It is very attractive and may be placed in a more prominent position in due course.

In the Vicar's Letters of July and August, 1934, he appeals to the congregation in these words:-

> *"There remains an excellent opportunity for someone to complete the effort (that is, the subscription list) with a handsome carved oak Font Cover. We have a quite handsome design in carved oak, the cost of which will be £50."*

No further hints were necessary and the Font Cover was provided!

It is worth mentioning that during the Diamond Jubilee Year it was agreed that a record of past Vicars and Churchwardens should be displayed. This took the form of a handsome oak board which is still kept up-to-date and can be seen on the wall in the foyer.

During the next 10 to 15 years further gifts were made to the church and faculties were obtained. Three of these were acknowledged in the Parish Magazine at the time. In 1942 Mr. Edgar Lobley presented a cross which was placed on the Reredos above the Holy Table. On the 11th November 1945 the Bishop of Penrith dedicated a Memorial Chalice and Paten donated by Miss Taylor, daughter of the late Rev. William Taylor, Vicar of St. Paul's 1920 - 1940 in his memory.

A further gift from Mr. and Mrs. C.C. Waddington, in memory of their son, Teddy, was dedicated by the Vicar. This took the form of a solid silver alms dish, simple in design and bearing the inscription "In loving memory of Flight-Sergeant W.E. Waddington, R.A.F. killed in action March 6th 1943, laid to rest in Military Cemetery, Dusseldorf."

The next major change in the furnishings of our church was perhaps an aftermath of the Second World War when many things had been shelved or neglected. The Church Magazine of February 1946 states quite simply "Our church is in desperate need of decoration and the P.C.C. have asked Mr. Hicks of Newcastle, a well known Ecclesiastical Architect, to prepare a scheme."

The scheme was accepted and a faculty obtained and in 1948 the work was put in hand. Mr. Hick's comprehensive survey envisaged a major transformation to the decoration of the whole interior of the church with special attention to the outlay and furnishings of the chancel. The main feature of the scheme was to whiten the interior additions authorised by the faculty were comprehensive. The brass communion rail was replaced by an oak rail given by Sir John Fisher.

A new oak lectern to replace the brass lecterns was the gift of Mr. & Mrs. Timms in memory of their sons, Eric, aged 21, who died in 1931 and Denis, aged 23, who died in 1941.

At the same time Mr. Albert Baythorpe and his daughter Brenda donated the two Clergy Stalls in memory of Mrs. Baythorpe who died in 1948 and their son Flying Officer Albert Baythrorpe who was killed in action over the Pyrenees in 1944. Mr. Albert Baythrope's service to the Church is recorded on a plaque.

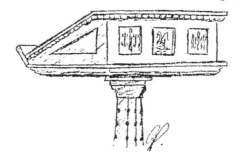

Oak Lectern

The church was closed for two weeks while the whole of the interior of the church was redecorated in white and the pews and oak furnishings were restained. The two commandment tables which were mounted on the west wall were taken down. The new memorial furnishings were dedicated by the Rev. Robert Nelson, Rural Dean, on Advent Sunday 28th November 1948.

This change in church decoration and furnishings was welcomed by the Vicar, the Rev. Arthur Briggs in these words.

"It was both pleasing and satisfying to get back into church for our services and to hold them under normal conditions."

However at the Church Council Meeting on 27th June he was placed in the invidious position of having to explain to the members of the council, how, without their knowledge, the choir stalls had been shortened to allow space for the clergy stalls. This, of course, had taken place before his Induction. The facts were that the P.C.C. had not sanctioned the shortening and the Rev. Norman Robinson had not petitioned for it. Unfortunately, Mr. Hicks, the Architect, had died since 1946 and his partner had to work on the only plan he could find, the original one which he understood to be the latest and official one. After this explanation the matter ended on a happy note.

War Memorial - Book of Remembrance.

On St. Paul's Day 25th January 1956 the Bishop of Penrith dedicated the lovely Book of Remembrance which had been beautifully illuminated by a member of our church, Miss Yates, and bound by the Barrow Printing Company in an embossed leather cover, also tooled by Miss Yates. This book has been placed in a fine glass-topped oak case made by Mr. Gilbert Caine of Dalton. The book records the names of those who lost their lives on active service or as civilians during the 1939 - 1945 war.

The Main Altar

As a result of the church extension in 1967 this book was moved into the foyer and is displayed below the 1914 - 1918 War Memorial Tablet which had been moved from the west wall.

Church Redecoration - from the Church Magazine Sept. 1958

The Vicar, the Rev E. J. Hay Hicks was advised that it was necessary to obtain a faculty before the church could be decorated. It was most distressing to hear that objections were being made at Carlisle. These seemed to be more related to the proposed renewal of windows rather than redecoration. We all appreciate the value of faculties to prevent controversial alterations. No-one could say that a clean-up was likely to cause controversy. Eventually the Chancellor's licence for this work arrived, thanks to the technical advice given by Mr. J. Parker, which cleared up any objections made by the Diocesan Advisory Board.

In June 1958, with the approval of the donor, Sir John Fisher, sliding bars were fitted to the Communion Rails and the rails fixed firmly to the floor.

In July 1961 an oak prayer desk was dedicated in memory of the late Rev. E.J. Hay Hicks. It was donated by his widow, Mary, and his children.

The Side Chapel

A most notable event took place in 1967 with the setting up of the Chapel in the South Transept. The Chapel was consecrated by the Lord Bishop of Tonbridge on the 22nd October 1967. The mass furnishings were funded by the Dunn Memorial Bequest which was set up by Mr. Charles Dunn in memory of his wife. He died in July 1967 and the Communion Rail was dedicated to his memory. The Holy table was carved by Robert Thompson of Kilburn, whose trademark, a mouse, is carved on a side rail. This table is a work of outstanding craftmanship. The Cross and the Bookstand were donated anonymously. It is most interesting to know that the Cross was made from the same seasoned oak which was used to rebuild the Hoses of Parliament after the Second World War. The Reredos Curtain was the gift of Mrs. Dorothy Birrell. The Vicar, the Revd. A. R. Fountain presented a Service Book in memory of his parents.

Voice Assistance - from the Vicar's Letter in the Church Magazine for November 1967.

"An anonymous donor has provided a very efficient and no doubt costly, Voice Assistance Equipment of microphones and speakers for use in the church. Many people have commented on the efficiency of this equipment and are most thankful."

Over the last 20 years the use of the Amplifier, Microphones and Loud Speakers have become commonplace although often a mixed blessing. Other gifts have been received to improve or extend the system and thanks have been recorded at the time. Recently a loop system has been installed in the front part of the church to assist members of the congregation using deaf aids. This has been greatly appreciated.

Commemorative Plaque A few days before Centenary Sunday 25th July 1971, a new plaque was affixed on the wall of the Church Foyer commemorating the church's first consecration on the 27th July 1871 and the dedication of the extended West End the 15th September 1976. The expenses involved in providing this plaque, beautifully carved and with gilt lettering in Vickers Workshops, were kindly met by Mr. John T. Cooper, in memory of his wife.

In my introduction to this chapter I stated that gifts to the church in the form of memorials are usually listed in the Terrier. Over the years many have been recorded in the Church Magazines and some are signified by the mounting of a suitable plaque and inscription. The remainder of this chapter is given up to a comprehensive list of these gifts and in many cases further details are given regarding the donors.

The stained glass windows are of particular interest because they were donated by families closely associated with the Parish at that time. I have devoted a separate chapter to the story of the East Window although other windows are of importance and interest.

The Chapel side windows were presented by the Robinson family and Thomas and Eleanor Ashburner (a family connected with the "fitting out" of ships built in Barrow).

The Baptistry side window was in memory of William Lesh of Newbarns who died 18th December 1888.

The side Sanctuary windows commemorate young men of St. Paul's parish who served in the First World War.

(1)Private Claud Sharp Jackson (23) who served in the Medical Corps of the London Scottish and was killed near Jericho on 30th April 1918 whilst dressing the wounds of another soldier. The window, the gift of Mr. and Mrs. Jackson, was unveiled at the 8 a.m. Communion Service on Sunday, June 30th 1929 by Miss Margaret Jackson. The window represents St. Luke, the Beloved Physician, and depicts his story of the Good Samaritan on the road from Jerusalem to Jericho.

(2)Charles Francis Preston, Town Clerk (1844 - 1907) as an expression of thanks for the safe return of his son, Francis N.D. Preston.

(3)Lt. Robert Cecil Staples who died in Mesopotamia on 13th May 1917.

The window above the Side Table in the South Transept is the "Mary Smith Memorial Window". Tribute was paid to her service with these words:-

"In Memoriam" October 25th 1924

Mary Smith. Aged 78 years.

Before St. Paul's Church was built, Mary Smith began her work in the old Schoolroom where Sunday Services were held, and when the Church was built 53 years ago, she became the first caretaker and verger, so that for close on sixty years she had spent her life in faithful and devoted service to St. Paul's Church and its people. The unveiling and dedication of the window is recorded in these words:-

"On Sunday, September 18th 1928, at the 8 a.m. Celebration, the beautiful little window in memory of our old and faithful friend, Mary Smith, was unveiled by her little grandchild, Kathleen Greenhow and dedicated by the Vicar, The Revd. William Taylor. The subject is "The Annunciation" and we think that Messrs. Shrigley and Hunt have given us a very delightful specimen of their work."

Other War Memorials were donated by families of:-

Captain Calvert Routledge (46) died in 1916

William Lewis Butler (22) died 19th April 1915

Geoffrey Lewis Butler (20) died 15th May 1917

In the Chancel two tablets record the life and service of two Vicars of St. Paul's Church:-

Charles Elrington Bisset 1880 - 84 who died 12th December 1888

Williams Berry 1896-1920 - who died 29th February 1920 aged 69.

Other furnishings recorded in Church Magazines and the terrier are as follows:-

The Church Organ donated by James Thompson of Monks Croft in 1900.

Panelling in the Sanctuary donated by Hannah and Joseph Huartson in 1927.
Church Wardens' Staves of Office - to mark the 800th Anniversary of the founding of Furness Abbey.

The Barrow Churches held a procession from St. Mary's Walney to the Abbey. The staves were first used in this procession and were the gift of the Churchwardens W.W. Waite and F. Fisher and bore the inscription:-

"1127 - 1927" Furness Abbey July 16th

The initials W.W.W. and F.F. are inscribed on the staves.

In October 1928 the Church received the gift of an old oak Sanctuary Chair. It is a copy of the famous Glastonbury Chair in Wells Cathedral with carved Latin inscription:-

"Give peace O Lord   To God be praise"

This was donated by Mrs. Brooke in memory of Mr. Brooke formerly Headmaster of Rawlinson Street School and a much loved and respected member of St. Paul's P.C.C. This chair was transferred to St. Aiden's Church in 1952.

The Organ hand pump was replaced by an electric blower in 1939 and was donated by Margaret Fanny Taylor in memory of her mother.

The silver Alms Dish, referred to previously, rests during services on an oak stand on the right of the altar. It bears the inscription

"In loving memory of Geoffrey Gregson"

and was donated in 1956.

The Vestry Clock was donated by (or in memory of) Irene Louise Beardmore in 1956.

A "Travel" Communion Set (in addition to the Prayer Desk noted earlier) in memory of the Rev. E.J. Hay Hicks was donated by his widow Mrs. Mary Hicks and family.

Other items have been given during the last twenty years and they are recorded here.

1973

Two troughs, for flower arrangements, in memory of Mrs. Dorothy Birrell.

A new microphone specially fitted to the Lectern for the reading of lessons. The gift of Mrs. May Richardson in memory of her husband.

A new reading desk fitted to the pulpit. This was given by Mrs. Higham and was purchased with the money which was given to her husband George, on his retirement after 22 years as Churchwarden. Sadly, George died before the cheque which had been presented to him could be used.

1975

Wrought Iron Flower Stand. The gift of the Mothers' Union.

Brass Christening Ewer to mark the 21st Anniversary of the formation of St. Paul's Young Wives.

It was decided to apply for a faculty to affix a Brass Plaque alongside the organ in memory of Miss Margaret Taylor's excellent service to the church, the reading of which would be:-

"In gratitude to God and in affectionate memory of Margaret F. Taylor
F.R.C.O., L.R.A.M. Organist and Director of Music 1922 -1975"

1976

Wrought Iron Flower Stand - the gift of Mrs. Smith in memory of her husband Mr. H.R. Smith.

Oak Tables in the Church Foyer - the gift of Mrs. Baty in memory of her husband Mr. J.S. Baty died 23rd July 1973.

1979

This item appeared in the Parish Post in 1979. It concerned Miss Dorothy Silverwood of 22, Hector Street who died at the age of 73. "We gratefully acknowledge the gift of a beautifully carved chair (made by her father) from the effects of the late Miss

Dorothy Silverwood and which her relatives felt she would wish us to have in the church. It has been placed on the Side Chapel Sanctuary."

1980

An oak flower stand attributed to the memory of Mrs. Dorothy Campbell who died on Sunday 17th February 1980. It wa made by David Caine of Dalton to match the wood in the church. Most of the cost of this stand came from a legacy left by Dorothy for the use of the Morthers' Union. An act of Dedication took place in March 1984 for this flower stand and also for a prayer kneeler given by Mrs. Emmerson in memory of her husband.

I hope that this completes the numerous and varied memorials and furnishings. In addition, the church has received many generous gifts of money in the form of donations and legacies and these have provided the means whereby repairs, renovations and renewals have been financed. At the present time (1991) the Church organ is undergoing a major 'operation' and the Church foyer is about to have an expensive repair and face lift. So, the "past" is financing the "present" and we thank God that their generosity enables us to do this.

CLERGY STALL

The First Phase of the New School

Principal guests at the opening of St. Paul's School new wing. Speaking is the Rev. E. J. Hay Hicks, Chairman of the Managers and Vicar of St. Paul's Church.

The Bishop of Carlisle with Mr. & Mrs. W. D. Opher at the Opening of the first phase of the School Building in October 1957.

Mrs. W. D. Opher opens the door of the new £10,000 wing of St. Paul's Junior School, Barrow, which was opened on Saturday. On the left is the Rev. E. J. Hay hicks, Vicar of St. Paul's Church.

Mrs. Opher presented each pupil with a badge representing the School blazer badge to commemorate the occasion.

The Opening of the New School

The opening of the completed School in September 1960. Clergy, Choir and guests await the arrival of the official opening party.

The Bishop of Carlisle (Dr. T. Bloomer) and Mr. Sidney P. Bundy (Headmaster) welcome the Opener Viscount Knollys.

L to R:- Mr. Sidney Bundy (Headmaster), Bishop of Carlisle (Dr. T. Bloomer), Rev. R. R. Fountain (Vicar), Alderman Francis Longstaffe (Chairman of the Education Committee), Mr. Ralph Jobling (Churchwarden).

Viscount Knollys is presented with the key of the School by the Architect, Mr. Gerald Jackson A.R.I.B.A. watched by Mr. George Warbrick (Clerk of Works) and Mr. Henry Hull of the Contractors Messers W. Hull & Sons.

Viscount Knollys turns the key in the lock to open the New St. Paul's School

Viscount Knollys addresses the assembly in the School Hall. Seated are:- Rev. A. R. Fountain (Vicar) Mr. & Mrs. W. Bate (Director of Education) and Mr. F. Longstaffe (Chairman of the Education Committee)

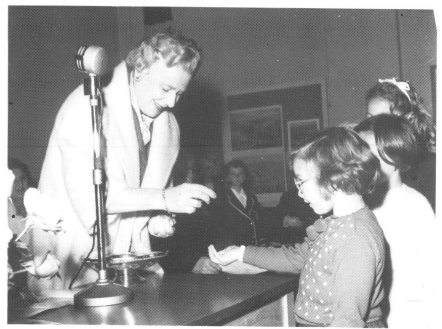

Lady Knollys presented commemorative badges to all the pupils.

An Oak Cross and Plaque are dedicated in memory of the Rev. E. J. Hay Hicks for his zeal in the erection of the school.

Barrow Blitz 1941

Land Mine on night of 3rd May 1941. Hill Road from rear. Next pair to No. 18.

High explosive Bomb on night of 3rd May 1941. Prospect Road and Hollow Lane

Crater in Hawcoat Lane seen from bedroom 3rd May 1941.

High Explosive Bomb on night of 7th May 1941. Undergreens Road looking W.N.W.

High Explosive Bomb on night of 3rd May 1941. Crater in Hawcoat Lane looking towards Throncliffe Road.

CHAPTER 4
The East Window

The colourful East Window in St. Paul's Church would certainly attract the attention of visitors if the town of Barrow with its public buildings, its churches and, of course, Furness Abbey was part of the tourist trail or the heritage trail. I wonder how many of our congregation gaze on this window and yet have little knowledge of its history or its significance. The singing of the Te Deum was at one time an important part of our worship. Many years ago the story of this window formed the subject studied by the pupils of St. Paul's School on their Wednesday morning visits to the church during Lent. They found it fascinating - I hope you do too!

Visit to Studio and Factory

On 21st September, 1928, it was stated in the Church magazine that:-

"The Vicar The Revd. William Taylor has recently paid a visit to the studio and factory of Messrs. Shrigley and Hunt, and seen the window in all the stages of its evolution, some of the larger panels being quite finished. It is a most wonderful and interesting process, and the window when erected will, we think, be one of the finest specimens of Messrs. Shrigley and Hunt's work. Indeed we are quite sure that the congregation will consider this a really magnificent improvement to the Church, as well as rejoice that our late friend will, in such worthy manner, be remembered in the House of God."

Unveiling and Dedication

This extract from the Church Magazine of 1928.

"We were delighted to see such a large congregation at the 8 a.m. celebration on October 14th, when the Archdeacon unveiled and dedicated the glorious Te Deum Window which now adorns our chancel. We were grateful too, for the beautiful address which the Archdeacon delivered at the service. To all worshippers in our Church the window will be a constant joy and delight, and what is more important, a perpetual lesson on the continuity of our Church. The picture of the Virgin Mother and the Infant Saviour is a copy of one of Murillo's paintings in the National Gallery, whilst the perfectly wonderful portrait of the Archbishop of Canterbury is copied from one at Lambeth Palace, and the robes were actually copied also by permission of the Archbishop."

THE EAST WINDOW
Description of the Window as given in the Church Magazine of August, 1928.
"We have the greatest pleasure in announcing that the large East
Window is to be filled in with stained glass. The donor of the window

is Mrs. Coulton Hunter, of Michaelson House, and the window will be a memorial to the late Mr. Hunter. We need scarcely say that we are delighted to have a memorial of our distinguished townsman and good friend in our church, and the more so because it will be a memorial worthy of him.

The design of the window has been approved by the Parochial Church Council, and we are now in a position to say that the Chancellor has approved of it too, and the Faculty will be passed at the next Consistory Court.

The window will illustrate the Te Deum, and the tracery above, Angels and Archangels, Cherubim and Seraphim, with the words "To Thee All Angels cry aloud," and in the central light at the top, Our Lord enthroned in glory (Thou sittest at the Right Hand of God) below in the same light, the Blessed Virgin with the Infant Christ (when thou tookest upon Thee to deliver man, Thou didst not abhor the Virgin's Womb).

There are three lights on either side of the central one: at the top of the three on the left hand, the Apostles, St. Peter, St. Paul and St. Andrew (the glorious company of the Apostles praise Thee); at the top of the three right hand lights, Isaiah, Jeremiah and St. John the Baptist (the goodly fellowship of the Prophets praise Thee); at the bottom of the three left hand lights St. Alban (the first British martyr, 4th century), Archbishop Cranmer, 16th century, and Bishop Hanington, 19th century (the noble army of Martyrs praise Thee); and at the bottom of the three right hand lights, St. Cuthbert, our own Northern Saint, Wycliffe who gave us our English Bible, and the present Archbishop of Canterbury, representing across the centuries "the Holy Church throughout the world".

The inscription below the figures will run as follows:-

"To the Glory of God, and in loving memory of Coulton Walker Hunter, who entered into rest, October 14th 1926. This memorial was erected by his widow."

The window will be unveiled and dedicated, all being well, on the 14th October next, immediately before the 8 a.m. Celebration; particulars of that service will, of course, be given nearer the time.

The work is to be carried out by Messrs. Shrigley and Hunt, of Lancaster, who are the makers of the other painted windows in the Church."

In connection with the introduction of the Archbishop of Canterbury's portrait in the window, the Vicar wrote to His Grace asking for his sanction, and received a most charming letter in reply expressing his complete approval.

Below is a copy of the letter received by the Rev. William Taylor from Randall Thomas Davidson, Archbishop of Canterbury. The Vicar of St. Paul's had written to the Archbishop requesting his permission for the panel in which the Archbishop is depicted. Notice the formality of his reply.

e.g. "Dear Mr. Taylor" and "I am.
Yours very truly"

R.Ð.C.

Lambeth Palace, S.E.1.

16th July 1928.

Dear Mr. Taylor,

In not a few churches which are adorned with representations of contemporary history I find that the figure of the Archbishop as such has been introduced, but to the best of my recollection yours is the first instance in which I have ever been asked beforehand whether I would sanction such a thing. Of course I can raise no sort of objection if the givers and makers of the Window are so disposed. On the contrary, I appreciate it entirely. I should not wish to say so publicly.

I am

Yours very truly,

The Story Portrayed

To illustrate the story portrayed on the window I have asked the help of the clergy and two members of our congregation to research and write a short passage about certain aspects of the story. I am indebted to the Rector, The Rev. Christopher Jenkin, the Curate, the Rev. Steve Osman, Mary Jenkin and John Hodkin for their contributions.

Te Deum laudamus "God, We praise you"

Latin hymn to God the Father and Christ the Son, traditionally sung on occasions of public rejoicing.

According to legend it was improvised antiphonally by St. Ambrose and St. Augustine at the latter's baptism, but has been more plausibly attributed to Nicetas, Bishop of Remesiana in the early 15th century.

Mary, the Mother of Jesus

"It was such a long and tiring journey to get to Bethlehem to register. My baby was almost due and I wondered at times if he would be born on the way; but I knew, really, that this could not be. The Scriptures had foretold that my baby - Jesus - would be born in Bethlehem, and so he was.

There were so many people there, all the inns and boarding houses were full; there was no room for us - until, that is, a kindly innkeeper took pity on us and allowed us to sleep in his barn. It was clean and warm, which was all we needed. My baby was born while we were there, and we had to put him in the manger on clean straw, because of course, there was no bed, but he was content and comfortable. I realised Jesus was special - that much I knew from Gabriel; but when we were visited by some shepherds we began to really understand. They said they had been told by a host of angels that the Messiah had been born, and they had been sent to Bethlehem to find him.

Their wonderment and humility was so real, so wonderful to see, they knew Jesus was the Messiah. I did too, of course, but I kept silent and stored all these things in my heart against the day when my beautiful baby would be a man, and must face very different men."

The Glorious Company of the Apostles

St. Andrew, brother of Simon Peter. Along with John, he was originally a follower of John the Baptist. Andrew was one of the first to respond to Jesus' call and he introduced his brother to Jesus. Very little else, other than legend, is known about Andrew.

St. Peter, one of the first disciples, he was given his nickname "rock" by Jesus as a sign of his future role as upholder of Jesus' teachings. Frequently seen as the disciples spokesman, and just as frequently seen putting his foot in it! However, he received special attention from Jesus and was the main leader of the early church.

St. Paul, the most effective missionary of the early church and its first theologian. Born a Jew, he was also a Roman citizen and fluent in Greek. Expert in Judaism, he was at first a persecutor of Christians. His conversion was marked by a revelation that Jesus was indeed the Son of God and led to his commission to preach to the Gentiles. Over 20 years of missionary activity saw the Christian church established throughout the whole of the Mediterranean area.

"The goodly fellowship of the prophets praise thee!"

(1)Isaiah: The verse quoted in the window is chapter 7, verse 14: "Behold, a virgin shall conceive and bear a son, and shall call his name Immanuel." This is one of the great prophecies of the Messiah, quoted by Matthew's Gospel, where we are told that "Immanuel" means "God with us".

Isaiah had a long prophetic ministry about 700 years before Christ; while many of his writings were primarily addressed to the situation of his own day, there were also great words which look forward to Jesus. Perhaps the most famous, apart from the "Immanuel" prophecy, are from chapter 53: "All we like sheep have gone astray; we have turned every one to his own way; and the Lord has laid on him the iniquity of us all." - a vivid picture of Jesus dying for us on the Cross!

(2)Jeremiah: Chapter 23 verses 5-6 read:

"Behold, the days come, saith the Lord,

that I will raise unto David a righteous Branch,

and a King shall reign and prosper,

and shall execute judgement and justice in the earth;

... This is his name whereby he shall be called: THE LORD OUR RIGHTEOUSNESS."

Jeremiah prophesied between 626 BC and 587 BC; he had an unhappy ministry, seeing Israel sink ever deeper into wickedness, seeing the inevitable divine judgement drawing closer - and yet being mocked, ignored, or persecuted for speaking out. In the end he witnessed the destruction of Jerusalem by the Babylonian armies of Nebuchadnezzar.

But many times he saw beyond the judgement to the restoration, and the coming King, descended from David, would reconcile sinful man with a Holy God.

(3)John The Baptist: The last, and, Jesus said, the greatest prophet; the cousin and fore-runner of Jesus. He is seen holding a scroll, with the words, "Ecce Agnus Dei", the Latin for "Behold the Lamb of God!" This is what he said when he saw Jesus coming to be baptised by him in the Jordan. Jesus was to be the final, all-sufficient sacrifice for sin - the Lamb who would be slain to take away the sin of the world.

The Noble Army of Martyrs

St. Alban Little definite is known of him, but he is believed to have lived in the third century, by tradition the first British martyr. According to Bede, he served in the Roman army and was converted by a fugitive priest whom he sheltered and with whom he exchanged clothes so that he was martyred in the priest's place. A church had been built on the site of his tomb by the year 429. The abbey of St. Alban was founded there and round it grew the town of St. Albans.

Thomas Cranmer 1489 - 1556 Archbishop of Canterbury from 1532 until his death at the stake at Oxford for alleged heresy in the reign of Mary Tudor. He was largely responsible for the abolition of the old church ceremonies, for the destruction of images and other relics, for the Book of Common Prayer of 1549 and that of 1552, as well as for the forty two articles.

James Hannington 1847 - 1885 The first Bishop of Eastern Equatorial Africa. He was consecrated in 1884 but was murdered in October the following year by the natives of Uganda when leading a hazardous expedition to open up a shorter route to Lake Victoria, Nyanza. He first went to Africa in June 1882 with six other missionaries, but fever and dysentery compelled him to return to England the following May.

The Holy Church throughout all the World

St. Cuthbert 634/635 - 687 One of the greatest English saints, he evangelised Northumbria, and was posthumously hailed as a wonder worker. In 684 he was appointed Bishop of Hexham, and a year later was transferred to Lindisfarne. He was buried there but his body was transferred to Durham Cathedral in 875 to protect it from Viking raids.

John Wycliffe c1330 - 1384 English theologian, philosopher, church reformer and promoter of the first complete translation of the Bible into English. He was one of the forerunners of the Protestant Reformation.

Randall Thomas Davidson 1848 - 1930 Archbishop of Canterbury from 1903 until 1928 the longest tenure in the office since the 17th century. He was noted as a commonsense moderate. He tried to reconcile extremists in the disputes between 1902 and 1906 over religious instruction in schools and the amount of ritual appropriate for services. He was active in the ecumenical movement and was President of the Lambeth Conference in 1920.

CONCLUSION

To appreciate the beauty and significance of the window, may I suggest that you take this copy into church and sit in the choir stalls and in the quietness and tranquility correlate what you read with what you see. Perhaps this will help you to realise that you and I are represented there:-

"The Holy Church throughout all the World"

What a thought!

CHAPTER 5

The Church Hall

In 1947, I was appointed Headmaster of the "New School". I accepted the position without taking the precaution of visiting the school. It was rather like a "blind date" as the interview took place during the August holiday. Imagine my shock when I paid my first visit in September by the kind invitation of Miss Gertrude Fallows, Head Teacher, to hear that the building has been condemned in 1939 and that some fundamental weaknesses were only too evident.

First of all it was not only a Day School, but also an evening Church Hall and a Sunday School. The Headteacher's classroom was also the assembly room and the church hall. The school clerk's office was behind a screen or behind the piano in this room and parents visiting the school during school hours were interviewed in the small doorway and porch leading into this room.

When the School Doctor, Dentist, or School Nurse made their visits, one class had to be absorbed into the other classes so that the children could be examined in the spare classroom.

This state of affairs was, to say the least, inconvenient and unsatisfactory. In a short space of time the School Managers were persuaded to convert the bell room on the Hawcoat Lane side of the school into a small office with telephone, and a larger area storing the heavy trestle tables used by the church for fairs, jumble sales, etc. and the stacking chairs, as well as storage space for the new PE apparatus which the staff were now able to use.

I quote this from the P.T.A. notes in the Church Magazine of November 1948, just one year after my appointment.

"The Essex Agility Apparatus, introduced to the Physical Training lessons this month, has proved very popular with the children. This useful apparatus, which can be used in the playground or indoors, aids the physical culture of every child in the school."

Each day, after 4 o'clock, the transformation from School to Church Hall took place. The high shutters which divided the main room into two classrooms were drawn back. The heavy oak and iron dual desks and seats were moved into a side classroom or double stacked at the side of the room. Books kept under the desks had to be stowed away in cupboards. Inkwells had to be collected.

The late Miss Madge Garnett, who was a member of the Fellowship Committee in the 1940s emphasises this situation in her short article on "The Church Fellowship in the Fifties" as follows

"In the Rev. Arthur Briggs' time, the present church hall was the day school. The Church Fellowship met on Tuesday evenings and before the meeting took place, the heavy school desks and partition between the classrooms had to be moved. Catering facilities in the school porch were very primitive with only children's wash basins and a gas boiler to heat the water. The programme for meetings was similar to today, a talk, a musical evening, a social and a religious evening. We were younger then and had more games and dancing. We used to invite groups from other churches and they invited us back.

One of the highlights was a Ladies Night when the ladies entertained the men with musical items, sketches, etc. and a similar Men's Night later in the session. Another regular was Fellowship Magazine when members with an interesting hobby or interest would give a short talk. In 1953 colour photographs became popular and we had our first slide show from Mr. Ken Norman. "The Anvil" is a programme which has continued since the Fellowship started.

We had some summer events. Golf at Rampside, Treasure Hunts, Tennis (at St. Paul's Court), Rowing on the Park Lake, Rambles etc. One memorable evening was entitled "The Mayor's Banquet" when an excellent three course meal was served. The guest speaker was the flamboyant and lovable Canon Nurse, Vicar of St. George's".

The Church Fellowship during the Ministry of the Rev. Arthur Briggs 1948 - 1953

This was the state of the Church Hall until 1957 when two classrooms were vacated as the younger children moved into the first part of the new school. This eased the situation and at this time a stage was erected at the south end of the 'main room'.

At Easter the remaining two classes moved - lock, stock and barrel into the new school, thirteen years after my appointment as "Headmaster of the New St. Paul's School". The old school then became the Church Hall. Quote from H. Hayhurst's book published in 1971:-

> "Considerable alterations were made to the building in 1961. The boiler had been converted from solid fuel to oil firing in 1960. The outside conveniences and dividing wall were demolished, and the porch and cloakroom at the south end were converted into a kitchen. The stage platform erected a few years previously was moved from the south end to the north end of the main hall and a proscenium added. The centre sliding partition was removed and a new ceiling fixed and fluorescent lighting installed. The belfry was taken down and one of the original porches converted into a toilet. The total cost of these alterations was over £1,500. Since then the extra repairs to the interior wall, new main windows and repairs to the roof cost a further £1,200."

The Church Hall and

Scout Headquarters Development

After a number of years of planning, negotiations, applications for a grant, disappointments and frustrations, a big step forward took place when in 1976 the St. Paul's Scout Group Council and the Parochial Church Council cooperated in the plan to build a Scout Headquarters and to refurbish the Church Hall. This was made possible by a grant from Cumbria County Council and D.E.S. (Department of Education and Science) of £15,000 for youth projects. A campaign of fund-raising was begun by both Church and Scout Committees. With this grant of £15,000, a low interest loan from the Cumbria Scout Council and money raised through donations, the Church Hall and Scout Headquarters were officially dedicated and opened in the presence of 300 interested members of the Church and the Scout Group.

St. Paul's Parochial Church Council & Scout Group
have pleasure in inviting

....

to the Dedication
by the Bishop of Penrith,
The Rt. Revd. W.E.A. Pugh, M.A.
and Official Opening
by the County Commissioner Scouts, Cumbria
Mr. J.A. Rawlings, O.B.E.
of the new Church & Scout Hall Buildings
11 a.m. Saturday 7th May, 1977
Coffee will be served from 10 a.m. - 12 noon

The two halls provided extra storerooms and were heated by a new Gas system. They were linked by a common kitchen with service hatches to both halls. The Scouts had an entrance on the east side but a common entrance facing Wheatclose Road led into a foyer with cloakroom and toilet facilities and double doors to each main room. This enabled the Scout Hall to be locked when necessary but available when both halls were required for joint events. In the March 1976 issue of the Parish Post it was made abundantly clear that the Scout Council had sole control over the use of the hall. I quote:-

> "Due to perhaps some misunderstandings, we want to say that the Church Council has agreed to the Scout Group holding a 25 yearlease of the new hall (this being one of the conditions of receiving the Government Grant of £15,000). This means that our Scouts have main use and control of the new hall but in mutual cooperation it will be available on special occasions for wider use by Church Organisations, who on their side, will not over-impose on the facility."

During the years since the opening in 1977,time and money has inevitably been expended on the upkeep of the halls. This has been very much the case in the Church Hall when efforts to improve the flooring proved a "knotty"problem. Valiant attempts to sand the floor by a team provided by the Probationary Service only resulted in the failure of the sanding machine and the continual protrusion of the knots. Finally, in 1989 a new floor was laid at a cost of £4,000.

The hall is still used by a number of Church Groups and outside organisations and is a great asset. In January 1990 and 1991 St. Paul's Guide Company staged two excellent pantomimes and provided new stage curtains and fittings. A permanently fixed screen which can be lowered and raised has now been erected to provide a better means of showing the many slide and film shows for the meetings of the Church Fellowship and other groups.

CHAPTER 6
St. Paul's School 1888 - 1917

Part 1

The writing of my series of articles on "The Church and the School" for the Parish Post was prompted firstly, by an article written for the January 1989 Parish Post on St. Paul's School 1947 - 1970 which described life in the 'old' school and the building of the 'new' school and, secondly by the idea of bringing to the attention of today's parishioners the history of the Church and School.

It could be of interest to know something about school life under each of the thirteen Headteachers from 1879 to 1991, particularly of those who served during the first nine years. Their period of office varied between 3 years 9 months and the much shorter period of 1 month - hardly enough time to 'mark the registers' and register one's resignation! It was not until 1st June 1888, with the appointment of Mr. Albert Joseph Helm, that the school settled down to longer periods of leadership.

I am indebted to the writers of letters and reports of Parish Events found in the store of Church Magazines which have been preserved. Another source of information has been School Log Books kept in the town's archives. These record events outside the normal routine, written, day by day by the Headteacher, and reveal, not only the trends and advances in education, the meagre supply of school materials, the visits made by the School Inspectors and Officials, but also the problems faced by Headteacher and staff working under conditions which would not be tolerated today.

The Headteacher's main concern was how to attain and then maintain, a satisfactory standard in the main school subjects, the 3 Rs, when faced by large classes, taught in many cases by uncertificated and untrained teachers. The staff in 1901 consisted of:-

Mr. A. J. Helm	Headteacher
Mrs. B. Cooke	Certificated Teacher
Miss J.E. Waite	Ex P.T. (Pupil Teacher?)
Beatrice Dickinson	?
Mary Ross	Pupil Teacher

Mr. Helm's difficulties increased through the frequent interruptions in attendance due to sickness, both of staff and scholars, and the occasional school closures for long periods due to epidemics. At random, I opened the Log Book and came across these entries for 1895 which fully illustrate the point.

1895

Jan 29th There are only 37 children at school this morning owing to a very heavy snowstorm. The registers are not marked but the children occupy the time in amusements.

Feb. 5th Many children are absent this week. I find that Mumps are very prevalent.

Feb. 7th No school possible today. The weather is very severe. The ink is frozen in the inkwells inside the school.

Feb.13th Mrs. '.....' absent again. We cannot get thoroughly to work owing to these breaks in the staff.

Apr.23rd School closed at 3.15 as the schoolroom is needed for the Parish Tea.

May 30th William Postlethwaite has been away 8 weeks. The excuse is potato planting.

June 10th Attendance is not very good as a few children have gone to the fair.

June 14th Two boys, F. Sims and F. Bennett played truant yesterday for which I punished them today.

June 28th Terrific thunderstorms - many children absent this afternoon.

Aug. 27th Stormy morning - attendance poor.

Sept.18th The attendance has been better this week than it has been for any time during the year.

There are many other references to attendance figures. Some quite serious e.g. epidemics etc., others refer to frequent absenteeism of staff, truancy of individuals or large numbers of scholars and many others because of occasional holidays granted for local or countrywide events.

1890

Mar. 1st	Relief of Ladysmith.
May 24th	Relief of Mafeking
Nov. 8th	Launch of Japanese Battleship "Mikasa"

School was closed on other dates for the launching of H.M.S. Vengeance, H.M.S. Euryalus, H.M.S. Amphitrite, and H.M.S. King Alfred. How the children got to Walney Channel to see these launches is not stated.

In 1898 a reference was made to the 'hiring fair' at Ulverston. Many years later in the early 1930s boys from my class at St. James's School attended these fairs and were hired as farm labourers.

1898

Jun 23rd Attendance not improved. I feel that several children have left, being hired, in some cases without the sanction of the local authority.

Cases of truancy are reported frequently:

1890

Mar.8th I find the two boys K. and M. Arnold are playing truant this week, and the parents do not seem to be able to make them come to school.

1891

Apr.24th Owing to the attraction of a circus procession the numbers dropped to 127 this afternoon.

1896

May 19th Eli Clark played truant today for which I punished him.

Other less serious reasons or excuses for truancy or official half-day holidays occur over the years.

1904

Sept 21st School closed today. Education Authority decided on account of a Wild West Show.

Mr. Helm served as Headmaster during the reigns of Queen Victoria (13 years), King Edward VII (9 years) and King George V (7 years), so naturally, important events during these reigns are logged, chiefly, I must say, because the school was closed to commemorate the occasions.

1901

Jan.29th Proclamation of King Edward VII (day's holiday).

1902

June 2nd Declaration of Peace (after Boer War) (½ day holiday).

June 20th Coronation of King Edward VII (a week's holiday).1910 May 9th Proclamation of King George V (children marched down to hear the Proclamation at the Town Hall).

1917

May 18th Visit of King George V and Queen Mary to Barrow. Children assembled at 9 am to march to their positions in Abbey Road.

June 13th Half day holiday in Commemoration of the Jubilee of the Incorporation of the Borough, by the wish of the mayor.

There is no record in the Log Book of the outbreak of the 1914-1918 War, possible because it occurred when the school was closed for the summer holidays.

The pattern of official School Holidays becomes clear as year by year they were taken at Christmas, Easter, Whitsuntide, and Summer (July-August). Occasional holidays granted on special days are also noted but two of these became part of the annual pattern. One was Shrove Tuesday. In my early schooldays we waited anxiously during the Tuesday morning session for the announcement that the afternoon would be free. At playtime we chanted these words:-

"Pancake Tuesday is a very happy day,

If we don't get a holiday, we'll run away.

Where shall we run to - up Biggar Lane

Here comes Miss Dobson with a big fat cane".

The 'message' always reached Miss Dobson and at 12 o'clock the good news came! The other holiday was given to celebrate Empire Day.

Here I turn again to the Church Magazine of June 1914.

"Empire Day and Peace Day"

"This was celebrated at the school on Friday, 22nd May 1914. Mr. R.F. Miller, a Sidesman, gave an interesting and patriotic address in great detail to the children on the British Empire and George V as their King. He emphasised that Mr. Helm and the other teachers are trying to help the young people to do their duty now. They were reminded of what was written in Peter 2, verse 17.

'Honour all men. Love the brotherhood.

Fear God. Honour the King'

If they did that, they would be doing their duty."

There was an adjournment from the Schoolroom to the Playground where the flag was hoisted and saluted and patriotic songs were sung and three cheers given. Then the teachers and children dispersed to enjoy their halfday holiday, which is one of the privileges of Empire Day".

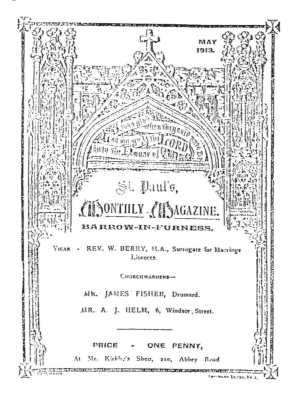

CHURCH MAGAZINE FRONTISPIECE FOR MAY 1913. MR. ALBERT J. HELM, FATHER OF MISS MARJORIE HELM WHO BECAME A MEMBER OF SCHOOL STAFF IN 1930, WAS HEADMASTER, CHURCH WARDEN AND SECRETARY OF THE CHURCH COUNCIL.

Part 2

There are a few instances logged under the heading "vandalism". These usually concern windows broken during holiday periods. The following entries record the administration of punishment which in later years would have to be entered in the School Punishment Book - a book open to the scrutiny of the School Managers.

1897

April 20th. I had to punish Mary Posnett sharply today for climbing through the porch window on Sunday and taking away an umbrella.

June 4th. I had to punish A. Bennett rather severely for striking at a teacher.

1901

Feb. 28th. Two shawls were stolen from the girls' porch. I am afraid they must have been stolen by someone passing.

1904

Sept. 21st. I had occasion to punish George Waite, brother of one of my teachers. When doing so, I was astonished to hear some very impertinent remarks from the said teacher, in the hearing of the scholars, questioning my authority. If such a thing occurs again, I shall ask the Managers to take very urgent measures.

Sept. 26th. School broken into. £1. 4s 10d was stolen and keys.

Mr. Helm had to attend the Police Court and on September 30th, this was reported:-

"A boy who had only been admitted a fortnight previously was found
guilty by the Court and received 6 strokes of the birch."

Meetings of teachers with parents were not a feature of school procedure at that time. Usually the parents appeared uninterested in their children's progress or lacked the confidence to discuss matters with the class teacher, and more so with the Headmaster. One instance reported in the Log Book is of a parent who did not conform to pattern and this illustrates the frustration that was felt by Mr. Helm.

1895 November 8th. A mother, Mrs. C, came to school this morning grumbling, the chief cause being that her children had not been "put up in the standard". Of course, her children, like all others, are placed where they ought to be according to their ability. This woman is a perfect nuisance and has given me more trouble than everyone else put together.

I have already mentioned the absence of individual children due to infectious diseases, but on at least three occasions, the school was closed when an epidemic occurred.

1895

March 28th. Owing to the epidemic of measles, the Medical Officer of Health has ordered the school to be closed until further notice. It was opened again after 5 weeks.

1907

November 25th. By order of the Medical Officer of Health, school closed until further notice because of epidemic of measles.

1916

April 4th. The Director of Education called at the school this morning, with instructions from the Medical Officer of Health to close the school owing to the epidemic of measles. (Closed for 1 month)

It was on September 21st 1916, when the first reference to medical inspections was made when Dr. Orr, the Medical Officer of Health examined the children. Then on June 29th 1917, it was reported that "Mrs. Pearce visited school today and tested the eyesight of the older children". These were the first steps towards the regular inspection of children's health, that is, a medical inspection at set periods in a child's school life - cleanliness inspections (the "nit-nurse" visits), eyesight and dental inspections.

Mention has been made of the Headteacher's concern over poor attendance and in March 1917, his feelings were summed up in these words:- "This has been a most unfortunate year for illnesses of teachers and children and hence have dogged our efforts all through." At the same time it was the duty of the School Managers and the Local Education Authority to ensure that registers were called and marked correctly before the morning and afternoon sessions. In 1895, the Log Book stated:-

"The registers must be inspected at least once a quarter at irregular intervals as requested by Paragraph 6 of Appendix II of Instructions to Inspectors. Attention is directed to Article 85(a) of the Code."

This rule was strictly adhered to and continued late into the 1930s when teachers of my generation will remember the Local Education Authority's Inspector, Mr. Fenton, visiting the classrooms with a critical eye on those whose registers were not correct and neatly marked.

1896

March 26th. "I called sufficient names on the registers to satisfy myself that they are correctly kept." William Berry (Vicar).

As an incentive, in 1905 a half-day's holiday was awarded to mark a good attendance.

1905

May 19th. By the instructions of the Education Authority, the school will be given a half-day holiday for having an attendance of over 92% in March.

This was the first of many "half-days" and in 1907 the Director of Education, Mr. Hawkridge, donated a shield to be awarded to the school with the best attendance.

School Readers –
90 years ago

Treasure Island

Ivanhoe

Children of the New Forest

Westward Ho!

Hereward the Wake

Nat the Naturalist

Water Babies

Swiss Family Robinson...

1907

August 13th. Messrs. Charnley, Hall and Hutchinson attended and presented the shield to the school for the highest attendance for the half-year ending July 30th 1907.

Large classes and a shortage of reading material is obvious from the Log Book entries from 1905 - 1919.

1905

March 31st. I exchanged 'Treasure Island' (84 copies) for 'Ivanhoe' (84 copies) with the British School, Dalton Road.

1906

May 7th. Received 40 copies of 'The Children of the New Forest' from Hawcoat School.

1907

January 14th. Returned to the Education Office 40 copies of 'Westward Ho'.

March 1st. Received 78 copies of 'Black Arrow' from Oxford Street School, but they were in such a bad condition and looked so dirty I do not care to use them.

September 5th. Received from Oxford Street School 78 copies of 'Swiss Family Robinson'.

1908

June 8th. Received from Oxford Street School 83 copies of 'Nat the Naturalist'.

These entries reflect both the need and the large number of books required, when most reading lessons were taught by "reading round the class" - not silent or individual study. Some steps were taken to add variety to the work.

1897

November 4th. The girls commenced to attend cookery lessons.

1899

June 17th. By permission of the School Managers, Mr. Morris gave a Temperance Lecture to the children of the Upper Standards at 3.10 p.m.

1903

February 26th. The Director of Education called to see about boys attending woodwork class.

May 16th. Boys commenced woodwork at the Higher Grade School workshop.

(On a site which is now part of the Ramsden Street playground of the Alfred Barrow School).

1915

April 21st. Miss E. Williamson of the Lancashire and Cheshire Temperance Union gave a Science Lecture to the Upper Classes.

September 1st. Classes III and IV took an Observation Journey this afternoon.

(Quite an intriguing title. I wonder how far they journeyed on foot and what they observed.)

1917

June 15th. Miss Richardson gave a Scripture Object Lesson on 'Alcohol' to the Upper Children this morning.

July 6th. National Baby Week. The Senior Girls attended the Exhibition.

Part 3

The outbreak of the 1914 - 18 War is not, as I have stated previously, recorded in the Log Book but the Church Magazine refers to it in these words:-

> *"The War in which we engage is one in which we enter with 'clean hands'."*

The young men of Newbarns and Hawcoat believed this, and subsequent issues of the magazine throughout hostilities published "Active Service Lists". List Number One contained 69 names; three from each of the Butler and Musson families. As these lists continued, they recorded the names of serving Officers and Men, Obituaries, Prisoners of War and Awards for Gallantry, concluding with List No. 47 in 1918.

"Your King and Country Need You"

Earl Kitchener of Khartoum Secretary of State for War

In July 1915 Mr. Helm, the School Headmaster, received a letter from Major Thompson which contained these words. "St. Paul's is well represented in this Battalion both by Officers and Men".

The Log Book and Magazines mention some of the efforts made by the school towards War Funds and War Savings.

In January 1915 the Church and School took part in a National Day of Prayer.

1915 January 3rd Day School and War Funds

"It is very pleasing to see the children of our Day School showing a spirit of patriotism and self denial during this time of war. Each week they cheerfully bring their "coppers" for the various funds and have already subscribed to the following:-

	£	s	d
Prince of Wales Trust	13	13	11
Princess Mary Christmas Box Fund	1	2	0
British and Foreign Sailors' Society	3	14	0
	£18	9	11

January 11th Day School

"It is pleasant to be able to mention the thoughtful action of two little girls, Edith and Mary Baines, who lately attended our school and are now living in the south of France. They have forwarded to the Master 2/6d each for the War Relief Funds."

1915 January 11th

"The school children forwarded a parcel of useful articles to the soldiers on Walney Island at North End Farm and were thanked by the Commanding Officer."

"The sale in aid of the Y.M.C.A. HUT WEEK realised £22. The children have certainly done well in their contributions to War Funds and show patriotism in a practical way".

November 15th

"Mr. Helm was excused School Duties to work at the Recruiting Office".

1916 August "War Savings. Mr. Helm has already got 75 subscribers in the school."

War Savings (in later years, National Savings) became part and parcel of Monday morning's work when "dinner money" and "Savings Stamps" were dealt with by class teachers and School Clerk. The school received a happy surprise in 1967 when the famous Coco the Clown presented a Certificate to the school to mark the fact that St. Paul's began a War Savings Scheme in 1916.   In September 1916 an unusual holiday was given. This was Munition Workers' Holiday (1 day) and the Education Authority closed all schools because "attendance would be poor".

In 1917 May 16th, school was closed early because it was needed for a Food Economy Meeting - a sign that in spite of rationing, food supplies were scarce.

In the same year on June 29th this interesting event occurred:-

"The 'Red Cross Ambulance' provided by the children of the Barrow schools, was brought into the school yard this morning and examined with interest by the scholars."

I cannot remember seeing the Ambulance in the school yard of Ocean Road Tin School, or of the main school which opened that year, but I still have a small ebony elephant which I won? or bought? as part of my School's effort to raise funds for this purpose.

Left to right: Mr. Hawkridge, Director of Education; Sir Alfred Barrow, Chairman of the Education Committee; Doctor Orr, Medical Officer of Health.

Part 4

During the early 1900s, the School Managers were obviously very anxious to keep the Church School at a time when more Council or State Schools were being planned. Every opportunity was taken to publicise that the standard of education provided by St. Paul's Church School was as good as, if not superior to, that given in the neighbouring Council Schools. One of the measures taken was to ensure that the building and its surroundings were maintained at the standard required by the Education Act of 1902, and to inform the parents of the parish, through the Church Magazine, of the need for improvements. This extract is taken from the April 1913 issue:-

DAY SCHOOL

"At a meeting of the School Managers on March 31st 1913 it was resolved to asphalt another part of the playground. This will absorb the balance in hand of the School Accounts. Some regular annual subscriptions are greatly needed. Notice is thereby given that collections at all services in Church on Sunday April 27th will be used for this purpose."

It goes on to appeal for all parents to accompany their children to church on that day or if unable, to send contributions by their children to school. On the occasion of the annual collection in aid of the funds of our Day School, the Vicar prefaced his sermon by explaining why these funds were needed. The collection amounted to £6. 6s. 2d, the highest collection of the month.

In the May issue of the Magazine, Mr. W.W. Waite, Borough Treasurer and Secretary of the School Managers supplemented the Vicar's preface in these words:-

"I am afraid there is an impression abroad that now the 1902 Education Act is in force all voluntary efforts can cease. This is not so. It is true that the teaching staff, books, apparatus, heating, lighting and cleaning, as well as the normal wear and tear of the inside of the buildings are provided for out of public funds, but the outside of the building, including the sanitary conveniences and the yard have to be maintained by voluntary subscriptions and Church collections.

We are therefore under a necessity, unless we wish our school to become a Council School, and so lose control of it, of raising funds annually toward the maintenance of the portions before mentioned. Two years ago the Managers spent £12 in asphalting a very small portion of the boys' playground, and now they must do another piece that will cost £15. The Managers would like, if they had the funds available, to cover the whole of both boys' and girls' playgrounds now, but as the cost would probably be £100, they are compelled to do the work in sections as circumstances permit."

This was followed by an explanation of the term "subscriber" and an appeal for subscribers at 2/6d a year for three years or a lump sum of £5 was made.(!!)

One significant improvement took place in 1914. On June 18th the scholars had been awarded a half holiday for good attendance, so it was arranged that a Garden Fete should take place in the afternoon to raise funds for the erection of a sliding partition in the schoolroom.

Other improvements were suggested by visiting Inspectors when they made their annual report on attainment of the scholars and maintenance of the building. This is a typical comment:-

"I am to enquire the intentions of the Managers as to remedying the defective ventilation in the infant classroom."

This was not a request but rather an order that things were put right before the next report. Obtaining funds for maintenance and repairs was the responsibility of the

Managers. In some cases money for these came in the form of Grant Aid from the Board of Education. Grant Aid was only awarded on the results of the Annual School Report which recorded the standard of attainment in the 3 Rs - Reading, Writing and Arithmetic. This report was forwarded to the Board of Education by its Inspectors and was really a system of payment on results.

Here are some extracts from these reports:-

In 1896 "The attainment of the school shows a decided advance since last year and if this is developed I shall be able to recommend the maximum grant under Article 10(a) of the Code."

In 1897 "The school continues to improve and is now in a very creditable efficient state both regards order and instructions."

In 1899 "Notice received from Education Department that a Grant of £40 has been approved for this school for the following purposes."

Increase in Salary	£
Headmaster	*20.00*
Assistant	*4.00*
Equipment and Repairs	
Painting	*16.00*
In 1900 Grant Aid	*40.00*
Headmaster	*20.00*
Assistant	*4.00*
Repairs to Roof & Playground	*9.00*
Desks	*7.00*

A turning point in the school's history occurred in 1917. At that time the Local Education Authority was reviewing the elementary school systems and the future of St. Paul's School was announced in the Magazine in these two paragraphs from the Report of Religious Instruction.

"Inspected July 11th, 1917

On Books 245   Present 217

One always anticipates with pleasure a visit to this bright and attractive school, and the departure this term of Mr. A.J. Helm, the Headmaster, to a neighbouring Council School will be viewed with much regret.

A reorganisation is contemplated in the near future owing to the removal of older scholars, and the school promises to consist only of Junior classes. This step is unfortunate, but it would appear unavoidable."

Mr. Helm's resignation followed and was reported in the Magazine as follows:-

(1917)PROPOSED TESTIMONIAL TO MR. HELM

Mr. Helm, as most of us know, has been appointed Headmaster of the Oxford Street Council School, and has sent in his resignation of his post as Headmaster of our parochial school as from August 28th, after a faithful and efficient service of 29 years. During this long period he has helped to educate the children of this parish, and it is difficult to estimate the influence which he has exercised on many who have reason to thank him for the benefits he has conferred on them. He has also taken an active interest in the affairs of the Church and Parish, and is now, as we know, Churchwarden and Treasurer of the Hawcoat Lane Sunday School. He has thus linked up the School with the Church, without any attempt to proselytise, and made it worthwhile for us to maintain our C.E. School. We are sorry to lose him as our Headmaster, but at the same congratulate him on his well-deserved promotion to a larger school.

We think it is most desirable that a worthy testimonial in the shape of a substantial cheque should be presented to him by the past and present teachers, parents and scholars of the school, and by the parishioners and members of the congregation in general, on leaving our school where he has for so long done such good service.

This was Mr. Helm's last entry in the School Log Book:-

1917 July 27th. The school closed today for the Summer Holiday. Having been appointed Master of the Oxford Street Council School, I relinquished my position as Master in this school, which I have held since the 1st June 1988.

It is interesting to note that 13 years later, his daughter Miss Majorie Helm commenced duties as an assistant teacher when school reopened after the summer holidays and retired 24 years later in 1954.

Memories of St. Paul's School 1911 - 1917

I have been fortunate to meet a former pupil of St. Paul's School who attended when Mr. Helm was Headmaster. This lady, a regular attender of St. Paul's Church, gave me the following impressions of school life at that time.

"I clearly remember my teachers, Mrs. Cooke, Miss Clements and Mr. Helm. We walked from Hawcoat Village to school and went home for dinner every day, the older children in charge of the five and six year olds. When my turn came to accompany my younger and reluctant brother, we were sometimes late because he stuck at Fox's Hill (the incline passing Mr. Fox's farm). We knew if we were late because Mr. Helm bolted the school door at 9 o'clock and latecomers had to wait outside until prayers were said. Then the door was unbolted and latecomers were each given two strokes of the cane. Boys who knew that they were to be punished for various offences usually pushed an exercise book down the back of their trousers before being told to "bend over". Other forms of punishment were to be made to stand in a corner or to stay in at playtime. (The wearing of a dunce's cap didn't seem to be in fashion).

I attended St. Paul's School from the age of 5 until I was 11 and my memories cover all that period. As a young child in the Infant's Class I had been accustomed to having a nap at home. This was not the right thing to do in school and I was brought back to reality on receiving a tap on the head by the teacher's thimble.

In the classroom we sat on long forms at desks with pot inkwells. The lessons were formal and we concentrated on the 3 R's, repetition of tables and spelling. We attended church on Holy Days. During the year we went on nature rambles to collect acorns, sycamore wings and specimens of flowers and leaves for identification in the classroom. We also visited George Romney's cottage to see a display of paintings, after which an essay was expected.

Another memory is of the class singing "London Bridge is Falling Down", of being on the end of the line, and being pushed over by the other children swaying. Of course, I got the blame and the punishment.

We had few visitors, but I remember a gentleman from the Education Office who counted the children present, checked the register, and visited the homes of absentees.

Happy Days!

CHAPTER 7
St. Paul's School 1917 - 1931

Mrs. Cooke

The School Managers had no hesitation in appointing Mrs. Cooke as the successor to Mr. Helm. She had served as an Assistant Teacher for 21 years and had given considerable support to Mr. Helm over this period of years. So on August 7th 1917 we read these words in the Log Book.

> *"I Bessie Cooke commenced my duties as Head Mistress of this School today."*

The School was now a Primary School and the Head Teacher had to concentrate on the problems arising because of the changeover. Illness of pupils and staff were, as before, a hindrance to progress but gradually they settled down and reports from both His Majesty's Inspectors and the Religious Education Annual Report showed that a standard was being attained and maintained.

Although the war was over it is interesting to note that on March 5th 1918 the school was closed for a week as the premises were needed for the distribution of Ration Cards.

On July 5th 1918 the school was closed until after the Summer Holidays on account of an epidemic of influenza. This is the first mention of "flu" and older people will recall that the epidemic was most severe and affected the whole country. Closure happened again from October 23rd to November 18th for the same reason.

In March 1918 this entry is quaintly put "Classes II and III took a short journey this morning in connection with the lesson "Leaf Buds." Other interesting items reflect changes in the school pattern.

1919

July 1st. School closed early to allow the children to attend "Bostock's Menagerie."

As most children had only seen wild animals in a picture in a book, this was an experience and pupils from most schools, including those on Walney Island, found their way to the Menagerie which was held in the Newbarns area.

1922

December 14th. Mr. Robertson, the Drill Instructor, visited the school this afternoon and took the children of the III and IV for Drill.

A Board of Education Syllabus for Physical Education came later for all schools although regular P.E. lessons using wall bars, ropes, vaulting horses etc. had already reached the Municipal Secondary School.

1925

September 30th. Standard V girls visited the "Palestine Exhibition" in the Victoria Hall.

This was of great interest to most schools as it combined the study of geography, history and scripture.

1925

November 24th. The school was open to the public this afternoon. 890 people visited the school including the Chairman of the Education Committee.

This is the first mention of an "Open Day", a feature that became an integral part of the school year. It was five years later when this invitation was repeated.

1930

July 17th. I invited the parents of the children to come and see the work this afternoon from 2.30 to 4 o'clock. About 90% accepted the invitation.

This was repeated in 1931 - again with an attendance of 90%.

There were probably other occasions when parents visited the school to see the Headmistress or Staff. In October 1921 the Vicar was rather anxious that an open invitation should be made. In the Church magazine he wrote:-

> "We find that by some unaccountable means an impression is abroad that our School Buildings are unhealthy. This is quite wrong, as anyone can see who will take the trouble to pay a visit to the premises. The Headmistress, Mrs. Cooke will be delighted at any time to show parents round. The School has recently been inspected by the Health Authority and no complaints were made. We hope that our parishioners will refute these erroneous impressions and help in all their power to make our Day School the great success we want it to be. Let us remember that it is the oldest existing school in the Borough having been in existence for some seventy years.
>
> Rev. W. Taylor"

This desire to uphold the standard of attainment in the school and the schools' good name, is reflected in the frequent reports of His Majesty's Inspectors. One of these, which took place in October 1926 stated:-

> "The School which now contains 120 pupils is staffed by the Headteacher and three Assistant Teachers. It no longer provides for boys above Standard II and for girls above Standard I. The older boys usually proceed to the Local Senior School, while the majority of girls on completing Standard I enter a Secondary School. There is a spirit of happy activity throughout. The teaching is bright and earnest, the children are alert and interested and the general results of the teaching and learning are very creditable."

Another report in May 1928 refers to the pupils' successes in gaining Scholarships to the Municipal Secondary Schools and goes on to say:-

> "It is clear from the children's happy demeanour in both classroom and playground that they are enjoying school life."

The allocation of children to Secondary Schools known in the 20s and 30s as the

Scholarship Examination, also showed that the pupils of St. Paul's, as well as the nearby Council School, were being well taught. I received the following letter from one of these "Scholarship Girls". She adds a little humour by signing herself "Clever Girl."

"I was a pupil at St. Paul's C. of E. School from 1920 - 1926. It was a small school with four classrooms. There were four teachers - Miss Martin, Miss Clements, Miss Hindle and Mrs. Cooke was the Headmistress. As an Infant, Miss Martin was my teacher. Two things I remember about then was Miss Martin buttoning up our coats at hometime and singing "Now the Day is over" before we went home for tea. I had a long walk to school and back twice a day in all weathers - no buses and no school meals.

Two of the classrooms were divided by a sliding partition and they could be used as one large room for special occasions, such as parties and concerts.

Mrs. Cooke's class was the last one at St. Paul's before going on to a Senior School. If one was clever enough the reward was a free scholarship to the Secondary School.

We sat at long desks which had grooves for pens and pencils and holes for the inkwells and we had to sit boy - girl alternately. Mrs Cooke had a long thin cane which she only used when necessary. She was strict on discipline, honesty and good behaviour, but she was respected and loved by all.

"Clever Girl"!"

During a conversation with "Clever Girl", I heard more about the 'walk to school' which was from Newbarns Village, up the narrow Strawberry Lane (now Hollow Lane) with its high sandstone walls on one side and fields on the other. She described visits to the school before the starting age of five so that Infants became familiar with the new surroundings. Playtimes, of course, remain in the memory and she said that the girls, at least, were pleased to have their own playground as many didn't like having to sit next to a boy and took every opportunity to move close to their girl neighbour if the boy next to them was absent or left the room. Penmanship was taught with pen and ink, although she remembers slates and slate pencils in the Infant class.

On April 30th 1926 the School Managers gave a half day holiday in honour of the girls who had won free scholarships to the Municipal Secondary School. All the girls who sat the examination passed. One girl obtained second position in the town, one third and one fifth.

The Church Magazine of July 1931 has this to say about examination results:-

"Once again it is our proud delight to announce the results of the George Moore Scholarship for which a large number of Barrow children sat and which is competed for by the schools of Cumberland, Westmorland and part of Lancashire, that out of the four Scholarships awarded to Barrow three came to St. Paul's School and the fourth to a former pupil now at the Grammar School."

This success prompted the School Managers to give the school a half day holiday.

It is obvious from reports received from His Majesty's Inspectors and Diocesan visitors that this emphasis on attainment was also accompanied by a happy atmosphere in the classroom. One report noted that there were 140 on roll but that the attendance was poor due to whooping cough and a Tradesmen's Holiday. It goes on to say:-

"Mrs. Cooke continues to conduct her school upon highly pleasing lines and excellent progress is being made. The utmost geniality and friendliness prevails and one is always glad to make the visit. Pictures have been obtained since last year."

A year after Mrs. Cooke's appointment, the Great War came to an end with Armistice Day on November 11th 1918. Celebrations of this event did not take place until 1919 when on July 17th the school was closed for Peace Celebrations and on October 24th the school was closed for "Peace Celebration Holiday". What form the celebrations took is not recorded in the Log Book or Magazine. In 1920 a War Memorial Fund was set up and on July 2nd a half holiday was given in the afternoon and a sale, on behalf of the Fund, raised £10.

The following year on Armistice Day, the children of Standard IV were taken to the park to witness the unveiling of the Cenotaph.

In the next few years holidays were given to mark other special occasions.

1922

Feb 28th A day's holiday in honour of Princess Mary's Wedding.

1923

April 26th A day's holiday in honour of the Duke of York's Marriage.

1927

June 29th A holiday given today due to the visit of the Prince of Wales. The children were taken to the park to see him.

1928

Feb. 6th School closed today to mark the funeral of Sir Alfred Barrow.

On a happier note, on November 9th 1928 a half day's holiday was given by the newly elected Mayor Alderman John Whinnerah, Chairman of the Education Committee.

In October 1928 the first Mid-Term Holiday was recorded.

In previous chapters, school closures due to epidemics of measles and chicken pox have been mentioned. Scarlet Fever cases were reported over the years but in these instances individual families who had been in contact with the disease were excluded from school.

1929

Jan. 29th The attendance is very poor - 55% due to an epidemic of Chicken Pox and Scarlet Fever.

Jan. 30th Dr. Orr visited the school and examined every child.

Feb. 1st School closed at 3 p.m. to allow men in to spray it. As ordered by Dr. Orr.

I imagine that caused a lot of concern when the news reached home. The Schools Medical Service increased its activities during these early years but it was not until April 27th 1920 that the School Dentist examined the teeth of all children in the school, aged 6, 7 and 8 years.

Two other developments in school life occurred at this time. The first was recorded in the Log Book on November 9th 1926. "The children of Standards IV and V were taken to the Theatre this afternoon to see the play 'As You Like It.'" A Theatre Company performing Shakespearian plays made annual visits to the Royalty Theatre in Cavendish Street.

The second development was the introduction of the Inter-School Sports in 1926.

1926

July 5th The school was closed this afternoon and the upper children were taken to the Secondary School's playing fields to run the heats, prior to the Sports Day on July 17th.

These Sports were to be a feature of school life for many years to come.

The training of teachers had obviously improved over these years and college trained teachers and uncertificated teachers with adequate experience gradually replaced the pupil teachers of Mr. Helm's era. Two interesting appointments were made. On June 2nd 1919 Miss Ella Martin commenced her teaching career at St. Paul's and she and Miss Majorie Helm who was appointed in April 1931 served the school until 1954. Miss Martin for 35 years and Miss Helm for 24 years.

The Local Education Authority had a system of pre-college training whereby young men and women from the Municipal Secondary Schools taught as Pupil Teachers under the supervision of the Headteacher and qualified class teacher. Other local teachers and college students were also given school experience.

From the Log Book:-

1926

September 10th. Miss Gladys Melville from Bingley Training College commenced a fortnight's "school practice" during the college holidays.

September 24th. By permission of the Director of Education, Miss Lynam, Assistant Mistress from St. Columba's School has been here today observing methods in the Infant Class.

1928

July 14th. Miss Edna Gough, a student from Stockwell Training College commenced two weeks teaching practice.

August 27th. Miss Caroline Hodgson, who is entering Warrington College in September commenced a week's teaching practice.(Miss Hodgson lived at Malvern House, Newbarns Village and was a former pupil of St. Paul's School.)

In 1931, Mrs. Cooke notified the School Managers that she was retiring. In the

Church Magazine the Vicar expressed his regret and also the appreciation of her services in these words:-

> *"It is with the profoundest regret we have to record this month the retirement of Mrs. Cooke after 34½ years service - 21 years as Assistant Teacher and 14 years as Headmistress of St. Paul's School."*

After referring to the successes of the school and the high tradition attained, he continues:-

> *"In Mrs. Cooke we have had a perfectly wonderful and delightful personality with little children. The children are happy and learn with the minimum friction, whether of naughtiness or idleness, and this is not a little owing to the motherly and wise guidance of Mrs. Cooke, so that they do not merely absorb knowledge but are encouraged to love learning for its own sake."*

In the School Log Book, Mrs. Cooke puts it very simply:-

1931 September 30th. As I am retiring I relinquish my duties as Headmistress of the school today."

Memories of St. Paul's School

By

J.S. Taylor, 96 Rating Lane, Barrow.

I attended St. Paul's School from September 1926 until July 1932. When I started, the four teachers were:- Miss Martin, Mrs. Hindle, Miss Doling and Mrs. Cooke.

The year I left the teachers were:- Miss Martin, Miss Helm, Miss Cummings, and Miss Fallows. This was a wonderful team and remained so for many years, and I was fortunate to be associated with them for all those years at the School, and in their retirements.

Miss Martin, my first teacher and probably my favourite, was a devout Christian lady, who had the gift of making her teaching so interesting that we all became enthusiastic.

On the very first afternoon, we were introduced to handicraft - when we cut shapes of animals which she had drawn on thin sheet cardboard. This was our first experience with scissors and soon the job in hand became tedious, and whilst Miss Martin was across the other side of the room, Ernest Browne and myself cut each others hair. Caught in the act, we were both marched off to Mrs. Cooke in the big room. "You are very naughty boys - hold out your hand" - one wallop with the cane - which did not hurt, but we pretended it did! In disgrace we both had to stand behind a blackboard and easel - one at each end of the room - and we remained there through play time and up to home time (probably 90 minutes).

My Mother, with brother Bernard in the trolley, collected me at 3.30 pm and being told of my performance, I suffered verbal abuse all the way home along Wheatclose Road, which was a very long way. My Father did not seem interested in my first day at school - but the following morning he took a photograph of my hair cut for posterity.

As far as I can remember, the cane had no effect on me. Perhaps I never cut Ernest

Browne's hair again, though the last time I saw him he could have done with a trim.

Miss Martin came from Millom; this proud fact she told everyone, and to illustrate this point, she would draw the picture on the blackboard. Black Coombe in the background, small sketches of houses in the foreground, Millom Ironworks, and a train on its way to Barrow. We all copied this and made our own improvements - some with a sketch of Miss Martin waving to us from the train. I was very proud of my own effort and it was hung on the wall for several weeks.

I remember years later when I was in our Chemist's shop, a lady and her young son called to collect some medicine; before leaving they unfolded a large piece of paper showing the boy's handiwork. I was able, to their absolute amazement, to tell the boy - "Your teacher is called Miss Martin and she comes from Millom". I wonder what she did with all those 'masterpieces'.

After a full week at school, the novelty soon wore off. I developed a limp, and faked illness; in fact any excuse not to go. I was therefore bundled into the car, and on arrival frog marched to Miss Martin who held me captive until home time.

About this time my Mother, I suspect, was in collusion with William Case from Manor Farm. He would call for me every day - and we both would walk up the road sucking sugar pigs he had brought as encouragement. I have known William Case as a true friend all my life and I was saddened by his recent passing. At his funeral I recognised many "St. Paul's faces" who I could name, and who I had known for some sixty five years.

My brother and I have always been grateful for the wonderful start and guidance we received at St. Paul's. When my two sons attended, I was delighted they were to have the same chances as I had, and at this time I was able to re-live through them, the happy time I had at St. Paul's.

My granddaughter now attends the school and at various times it is my joy to collect her and listen to her patter on the way home. Perhaps she may do the best of the lot? I sometimes wonder!

May the School continue in its great work, and I wish all every success.

24th February 1992

Memories of Mr. William Case

The late Bill Case, formerly of Manor Farm, gave Mary Jenkin, the editor of the Church Post these `Memories' of the 1920's.

"In those days, Wheatclose Road was only half made up. Dane Avenue
had just a few houses. It was rough and unsurfaced all the way up - on
a windy day, the slag blew in your face. Horses pulled floats on iron
hoops rather than tyres, with candle-lamps for lights."

Mr. Case first went to a private school in Prospect Road run by his aunt. After six months, she gave it up in order to keep house for her recently widowed father, so he transferred to St. Paul's. He recalls that he still spent much time with his aunt and grandfather, as it was always hard to get his homework done at home! Among the staff of those days were Mrs. Cooke the head-mistress, whose ambition was always to get the entire top form into the grammar school; and Miss Martin, in charge of the infants and who was still there a generation later. Miss Martin used to come on the train from Millom and catch a tram up Abbey Road. This was the period when the first "bus" - a single-decker - was introduced by the Borough. Mr. Case even remembers the driver's name!

In the morning, there was regularly a line of fifteen or twenty children waiting to be caned for being late. But strictness can go with generosity; from time to time, there were handouts of clogs to children of unemployed fathers. There were no school dinners. Most children went home to eat but some brought sandwiches and tea was brewed for them in school.

Mr. Case recalls a number of his fellow pupils of those years, but the memory is tinged with sadness for many of them were lost in the war.

REMINISCENCES FROM CLARICE ROZZE

(NEE GILLBANKS)

"I went to St. Paul's Junior School in what seems to be 'the long ago' or certainly in the olden days in the eyes of to-day's pupils. It was 1921 that I embraced education for the first time at the old school on the corner of Hawcoat Lane and Wheatclose Road, and on reflection life was so much simpler than now.

Quite often we were chaperoned by our Headmistress, Mrs. Cooke when she had a string of infants on either side as we walked up, what was then commonly called Strawberry Lane - a lane with a high hedge at one side and trees on the other, and quite often we heard the warning cry "stand in the hedge and let the horse and cart go by!" As we grew older we tackled this perilous journey alone, or with a best friend; and sometimes a reluctant little boy who was a terror would escape at the soonest opportunity!

Miss Martin was our class teacher and she was lovely. We had sand trays to draw on and we had sums and letters and words and we were made to read. If you were slow you had special attention in a small room but most children read simple lessons before they went into standard one. Miss Martin used to make us Oxo or Cocoa (taking our own requirements). Standards one and two had the next room and Miss Donlan taught two classes.

We had desks - I always wanted one by the window but didn't always get it! If you were naughty you had to stay in and write a hundred words. We wrote 'joined up' writing of course - printing was for infants and for those who wanted to be infants! We had a story on Friday afternoons and I liked that - who didn't? We also had poetry-reading out loud - sometimes I didn't like the books -I didn't like "King of the Golden River". We did multiplication and long division and bills of how much everything cost.

We played in the playground on the asphalted bits - an odd game called "Captain Ball" with circles. The other parts of the playground were pebbled and very painful if you fell.

The Vicar, Mr. Taylor, used to come sometimes to see us and we all rose with a clattering of desks and the boys all bowed and the girls curtsied, and everyone was on their best behaviour for five minutes!

Most children went home for dinner; only a few brought packed lunches and were cared for by Miss Martin. Then after our Summer Term and tests which happened every year to see who was top of the class we went up one into Mrs. Hindle's class. She was quite nice but with hindsight she knew what was what and we didn't get away with too much - we didn't anywhere for that matter! We did knitting and sewing with Mrs. Hindle and drawing plants in pots, and ellipses and lines and geography and all sorts of interesting things.

There were some things that continued - every morning at nine o'clock - we had to be punctual - we had prayers. If you were not on time you got the cane so everyone made a great effort to be early - so nine o'clock for prayers and a hymn and then until 9.50 a.m. it was scripture. We had different kinds and it wasn't dull for me - it was good for us. We did some local points - Furness Abbey, Monks - St. Aidan, Columba, Bede, and Lindesfarne, and different architecture of churches, such as Norman, Perpendicular etc. then of course, we also did Bible Study - O.T. stories, and N.T. and the Catechism, the Ten Commandments, the Creed and every year we had the Inspector to test our knowledge - and did things hot up before he came! There were great efforts made to keep our standards up. All round the walls there were drawings we had done - the painful fruits of labours. I had, and I'm sure most children had, a pride in all this effort. We engaged our Mums and Dads in the search after knowledge.

My Grandmother bought me a Bible when I was seven and I could read it myself - coming unstuck at some of the big words!

May Day was a great day - we used to have a Maypole in the playground and do country dancing and sing. It was fun.

St. Paul's School Hawcoat lane/Wheatclose Road, seventy years ago.

Empire Day was a great day - similarly things happened with red, white and blue everywhere and with the piano outside.

Christmas-time was lovely. We made decorations - even though times were probably harder then, our Mums were great. We still had jelly, fruits, cakes - you name it, we had it - it was a good school and I'm sure it still is. We had concerts. On Feast Days we went to church and had a holiday in the afternoon - we loved that!

We were always trying to get 100% attendance - I don't know if we managed it or not. It was not popular to have a headache and stay off school when there was a drive on. Of course when one achieved the maturity of Grade 4/5 you were engaged in the 'Battle of the Scholarship'. One had homework with those weird and wonderful sums about baths and water! Do they still have them? Grammar was dealt with in a very practical manner and most of us knew our subject from our predicate when we terminated our education at St. Paul's in 1927.

I have the happiest memories of my life at this time, and now I look back and feel very grateful for the care and attention that was given to us in those days. I feel the conscientious teaching and kindness of those four ladies laid a foundation which has stood me in good stead all my life - and not merely for spelling, sums, and academics but for the recognition of all that is good in life. I feel that I owe a debt of gratitude to St. Paul's School which I am pleased to be able to record.

Pupils of St. Paul's School c.1927
This Photograph has been loaned by Mrs. Christine Thompson whose husband, the late George Thompson is fourth from the left on the front row (shading his eyes). Their children, Ian and Sheila, were pupils in St. Paul's New School in the nineteen-sixties.

CHAPTER 8

St. Paul's School 1931 - 1947

When Mrs. B. Cooke announced her retirement, the School Managers had no hesitation in naming her successor.

Mrs. Cooke's Successor

"The Managers have appointed Miss Gertrude Fallows, at present Chief Assistant at the Oxford Street School as successor to Mrs. Cooke. The Managers are of the unanimous opinion that they have found one who would maintain the high standard so long achieved by St. Paul's School and they wish her every success in her undertaking. They feel sure that she can count upon the loyal and enthusiastic cooperation of her staff."

With the appointment of Miss Fallows the history of the school reached perhaps its most important phase, with the exception of the building of the new School. Under Miss Fallows' leadership the school continued on the same lines with a stable and able staff, maintaining the high standards set by her predecessors in a happy family atmosphere. The following Report from the Diocesan Inspector confirms this.

"The religious teaching in this school easily ranks among the best in the area that comes under my notice. The four teachers are deserving of commendation on this year's work. Answering is given with a clearness which evinces an excellent knowledge of the subject and all the children can express themselves freely and naturally. The year's work is made largely to centre round the Church seasons and festivals and the staff all aim at giving the Church's teaching to the Church's children, in the form which enables it to be put into practice in their school life. A most impressive opening service and very clear, enunciation and singing is a pleasing feature.

I have seldom seen better descriptive and illustrative work done, and the composition and memory work generally is of the same good standard.

The syllabus is well drawn up and all that is done is done well, and a true and devout tone pervades the work throughout".

In 1941 Miss Fallows wrote two articles in the Church Magazine on the "History of the School". The first article was factual and covered the period up to 1931. The second article was headed "St. Paul's School Today". Here she gave details of the school, numbers on roll, staffing etc.. She has this to say about the staff.

"This is a very happy school and the staff consisting of Miss Fallows, Miss Martin, Miss Helm and Miss Hayes work most loyally and enthusiastically to give of their best in the interests of the children. Personnel of the school has for many years consisted of teachers who have been thoroughly trained in the teaching of the Church. Miss Fallows and Miss Martin hold the Archbishop's Certificate in Divinity, while Miss Cummings who recently retired, and Miss Helm, have had long experience in Church Schools."

In the same article, after explaining the efforts made to integrate the School and the Church through scripture lessons, school assemblies and visits to Church during Lent she has this to say about class subjects.

"The Class Subjects receive in order individual care and attention. English is the basis subject in the School. Handwork, Art, Needlework, History, Geography and Arithmetic are all worked on the lines set down for the modern Junior School. Country Dancing, Rhythmics, Physical Training and Games are all taken but under crippling conditions. Music, consisting of Singing and Percussion band work help in the leisure side of school life.

The training of our children is arranged to give a real Christian upbringing, which is the essential foundation for success and happiness in life. Our School forms a most vital and important link in the chain of our Parish life and one worthy of the support and co-operation of the parishioners."

The Church Magazine, now under a new title "St. Paul's Journal", contains reference, year by year, to the Harvest Festival Services held in the School. This extract is from the Journal of 1932.

"A delightful Harvest Festival was held in our school on September 22nd - A short half hour, with harvest hymns and prayers. The generous offerings of the children included about 150 eggs and fruit, vegetables, cakes, pots of jam, etc. and required two motor cars to convey them to the North Lonsdale Hospital. The children enjoyed the event hugely and the Matron of the Hospital was naturally delighted with such a large and useful addition to her larder."

During Miss Fallows' period as Headmistress, further efforts were made to open the school to the parents by the production of Christmas concerts and eventually an annual Nativity Play. In 1943 a parent wrote this account:-

Christmas Concert

"With great pleasure I accepted an invitation to be present at the Christmas School Concert. The room had been tastefully decorated by the children and the scene presented was one of colour, brightness and gaiety.

The proceeds opened with an exhibition of folk-dancing, gracefully and cleverly executed by the senior girls and boys. This was followed by a performance of the percussion band by the infants and a charming little play entitled "Toyland". The children of Form 3 delighted the audience with their play "Kind Thoughts". Several scenes from "Snow White" were enacted by Form 2. The entry of the Seven Dwarfs, complete with axes and flowing beards, caused great excitement among the children and finally the play ended with 'he appearance of the dashing Prince who carries off Snow White.

And now the scene changed from one of laughter to a more serious atmosphere. The senior children gave a delightful performance of a beautiful Nativity Play. These clever little artistes had certainly caught the right atmosphere of reverence and solemnity, both in their elocution and movement. The singing of appropriate carols and the beautiful costumes added greatly to the performance of the play."

On the following two days, Christmas parties with games and a Hat Competition were held. At both parties everyone had a most unexpected and delightful surprise. Many boxes of sweets had been sent by the American War Relief Society and were handed round between the games. This was indeed a luxury when sweet coupons were needed to buy rationed supplies.

The annual Nativity Plays and Class Parties were to become a feature of school life for many years to come.

Another important innovation was the formation of the School Association - Parent Teacher Association. This Association was not primarily a fund-raising body but a means whereby Parents could meet the Headmistress and Staff and Clergy in the evenings for the mutual advantage of all. Meetings were conducted in a business-like way with the usual Officials and Committee elected at an Annual General Meeting. Some meetings were of a social nature but most were devoted to the educational topics of the day. For example, in 1944, Mr. S. Price, Headmaster of the Boys' Grammar School, who had two of his own children attending St. Paul's, spoke on the topic "Future Secondary School Development". In 1945, Mr. Shillito, Headmaster of Alfred Barrow Modern School chose to speak about "The Place of the Modern School in the new Educational Programme." Another parent, Dr. Forrest addressed the meeting in 1943 on the subject of "Health of Children" which was very well received and was followed by a lengthy question and answer period.

The School Managers were well aware of the problems facing the Headmistress and Staff, working in a building, which although imposing on the outside, was inadequate in many ways on the inside. With their limited resources, provided by the Church Council and the "School Subscribers" system, they did what they could. These extracts are taken from the Church Magazine of December 1931 and April 1932.

__December 1931__ During the Christmas holidays certain very necessary work will be done to improve our school. The window in the North Room will be enlarged and lowered to give more light and there will be further necessary improvements in the Childrens' Offices. The Managers do not wait for the Board of Education to demand these things; it has always been their custom to anticipate such needed improvements.

__April 1932__ At a meeting on February 12th the Church Council voted an annual grant of £10 to the Governors of St. Paul's Day School, towards the general upkeep of the School.

In August 1939, shortly before the outbreak of the Second World War, the School Managers received this highly critical report on the School Building from His Majesty's Inspector.

> *"The premises consist of three rooms, one of which is divided into two by a movable screen. The largest room was given temporary recognition for not more than 40 scholars in 1932 and it has continued to be used as a classroom since that date. There is no "free space" for indoor Physical Training and other activities now usual in a school for Juniors and Infants and the paved portion of the playground is so worn that outdoor Physical Training is limited.*

The report continues by commenting on the smallness of the rooms, the congestion of the furniture, the lack of ventilation, the inadequacy of accommodation in the Infants' Cloakroom and Lavatory and Storage and concluded by saying that the classroom floors were in urgent need of repair.

The Vicar's comments on this Report were as follows:-

"The enlargement of the school to satisfy these demands would be a costly matter for which we have no funds. We had already arranged to pay our share in the reflooring of the school, and the Local Authority had got out tenders for doing it in the holidays. This is now held over, and the Authority will not proceed pending the decision of the Foundation Managers of the School."

In October 1939, the Vicar, the Revd. William Taylor announced his retirement. War with Germany had broken out and the needs of the School Building paled into insignificance. I have been unable to find reference to these needs until May 1941, when Miss Fallows wrote:-

"During the air raids of May 3rd and 4th the school building suffered structural damage and was unfit for use until repairs had been executed."

The roof was mended, glass inserted in the window frames and the debris was cleared away. After this, the school re-opened and thankfully that was the last of raids.

The subject of repairs to the school lay in abeyance until 1945 when this extract appeared in the July Church magazine.

School Yard

"From time to time we have had complaints from parents and others with regard to the bad condition of our school playground which is the frequent cause of accidents and at the same time, very hard on children's footwear. The surface was a bit worn before the 1941 blitz, but the debris which was thrown in to the yard at that time caused the great holes which have become so extensive as to almost cover the whole area. We asked for repair and resurfacing at the time, but the licence was refused. We have applied again and again since then, but so far the work has not been considered sufficiently important or urgent to warrant a licence."

It goes on to explain that the School Managers have again asked the Chief Education Officer to make a fresh application for resurfacing. The cost of this was to be found by the Managers and not out of the School Appeal Fund. Three years later, shortly after my arrival as Headmaster, I was visited by Mr. Clay, one His Majesty's Inspectors of Schools and as a result the whole yard was resurfaced allowing games to be played on it with safety.

School Building Fund

In February 1944, the Vicar, The Revd. Norman Robinson wrote a lengthy article in the Church Magazine under the title of "The Church and the Education Bill." He outlined the proposals in the Bill for religious teaching and advocated that Church people should demand an amendment to the Bill sanctioning denominational teaching in all Church Schools, - Anglican, Roman Catholic and Nonconformist. He also stated

The Bill offers Church School Managers 50% of the cost of reconstructing their buildings to bring them up to the modern standard."

This offer sparked the Church Council, School Managers and Parents into a commitment to raise £8,000 with the 50% grant from the State making a total of £12,000 *"to provide a building and playground which will make for all round efficiency and supply the right environment for the training of the body, mind and soul, which is the true purpose of a Church School. We must aim high"*.

The School Building Appeal Fund was inaugurated by a "Day of Prayer and Gifts" on Thursday July 20th 1944. In September a Penny-a-Week collection scheme was started, supported by a voluntary committee with a team of collectors and helpers. This was the main means of raising money. Every house in the parish received a letter and support came from all denominations. From 1944 to 1948 numerous fund-raising activities took place and the following list from 1944-45 gives an indication of the wide support given by many Church Organisations.

The Girls' Friendly Society (G.F.S.) - A Sale of Work

The School Association - A Caledonian Market

The 21st Girl Guides - Part proceeds from Jumble Sale and Sale of Work

Some 'Ladies of the Church' - A Social Evening held in spite of a terrific snowstorm.

A Mothers' Union Garden Party.

The "Brownies Effort" - Concert by the Brownies followed by one organised by Mrs. Graham.

"V.J. Day" Street Parties - Celebrating "Victory in Japan".

St. Paul's Drama Group - Presentation of J.B. Priestley's Play "Laburnam Grove."

Dancing Matinee - Pupils of Miss Maud Tranter gave a delightful display of dancing in the School on Saturday April 5th 1947.

The School Appeal Fund continued until 1948 when the total reached £6,000 - £2,000 short of the target set in 1944. It remained dormant until 1955 (earning interest) when, under the leadership of the Revd. E.J. Hay Hicks the Church Council took action after a card referendum of the parishioners indicated that the time was ripe for the Appeal Fund to be re-opened.

Retirement of Miss G. Fallows

In 1947 I believe the School Managers were taken by surprise when Miss G. Fallows tendered her resignation. Everything seemed to be going well. As the Vicar, the Revd. Normal Robinson, reported in his address at the Annual Parochial Meeting:-

"The Parents' Association has continued its good work, providing a useful contact between parents, teachers and clergy, which is I believe, much appreciated all round. The School Building Fund has reached the splendid total of £4,350 in 2½ years due to the hard work of Miss Fallows (Secretary), Mr. Waddington (Treasurer) and the District Secretaries and Street Collectors."

Here is an account of the presentation to Miss Fallows in 1947:-

"On Friday 31st October, the School said 'Goodbye' to Miss Fallows on her retirement. She was presented with a beautiful petit-point dressing table set for which the teachers, the children and their parents had subscribed. Miss Fallows, in reply, thanked the School for their present and good wishes and asked to children to remember, above all, to be good Soldiers of Christ."

So ended another chapter of the School's history. Although Miss Gertrude Fallows had left the school, she served both school and parish in a secretarial capacity for a considerable time and, as the new Headmaster, I appreciated the help and advice she gave me in my first few years.

ST. PAUL'S SCHOOL - A Personal View

After an association with St. Paul's School stretching over nearly 50 years, the first surprise is to realise how long that sounds - it does not seem very long!

I recall my early days - infant classes with Miss Martin; the shock of being made to work by Miss Helm; Miss Haye's class and finally, two years with Miss Fallows - four teachers covering all the years, two with two age groups in the same classroom in what is now the Church Hall. The toilets were outside "round the back" in a separate building against the boundary wall where the Scout Hall now stands. There was a wall between there and the school. The boys' playground was on the Wheatclose Road side and the girls' on the other side!

After the "blitz", the School was so badly damaged that we moved into the Church - the infants in the vestry, the other classes in different corners of the Church - which also had bomb damage. Our next "home" until the School was made habitable was the Furness Cricket Club Pavilion.

The teachers were unchanged throughout my years - Miss Fallows retired shortly after I moved on and, over the next few years, Miss Helm and Miss Martin also retired after many years service. (Did Miss Martin really complete over 35 years at the School with only one day off, when the Railway was bombed and she could not make her daily journey from Millom?).

The School buildings were old and with wartime restrictions and limited teaching numbers, there may have been academic limitations, but there was a true Christian basis to the teaching and to the life of the School which I believe was even more important than just exam results.

We have indeed been fortunate that through the two subsequent headships of Sid. Bundy and Hilary Riley, that same Christian spirit has continued, actively supported by the clergy, over the years.

For many years I have been privileged to continue my association with our School as Treasurer to the Managers (now called the "Governors") and, in more recent years as a P.C.C. representative member.

There are again many changes afoot in the word of education and St. Paul's School will be affected in due course by the new style management. I am confident that Staff, Governors and Parents will work together with the support of St. Paul's Church to ensure that we have a thriving School, maintaining its high standards of education, Christian, academic and sporting, for the good of our youngsters over these most important years of their development.

JOHN WINDER

Photograph taken in September 1937, loaned by Denis Stanswood. Notice the display of Harvest gifts at the back. Front row:- Douglas Ellis, Eric Rogerson, Jack Dall, Colin Banks ?, Kenneth Mansfield. 2nd row:- Derek Dickinson, Marjorie Dodd, Colin Bell ?, Eric Atkinson, Mavis Lacey. 3rd row:- Denis Stanswood, James Pass, John Black, Ian Waddington, Clifford Scott, (6). 5th row:- Betty Charles, John Sangster, Eric Phizacklea, Pauline Roberts, Alan Langtree, June Shepherd, (?), Ronnie Rushton, (?) Derek Hinde.

Letter from Mrs. Peggy Hartley (nee Hayes)
to Rev. Stephen Wright.

I had the school very much in mind during late January; on St. Paul's Day I recalled the many times we had attended services in Church on that day, staff and pupils together, and realised that February 1st this year would be the fiftieth anniversary of my first day at the school as a very young inexperienced teacher.

I shall always remember the very warm welcome I received from Miss Fallows, Miss Helm and Miss Martin, and the subsequent guidance, support and encouragement from Miss Fallows. Yes, I shared that large room with Miss Fallows for nine years - separated by a glass partition - each with two separate classes to teach and several "streams".

So many pupils come to mind. Not to be forgotten - Mrs. Greenhow arriving daily on her bike to clean the school and, during the war, to serve the dinners which arrived in large containers each day.

On the evening of May 3rd 1941 both the school and my home in Wheatclose Road were severely damaged. I was temporarily redeployed until the school was repaired and the roll restored. Together again school life continued as before. There was always a wonderful feeling of family within the school - pupils, staff and parents, working together towards a common goal inspired and led by Miss Fallows.

In later years I taught in larger, more modern schools with wonderful buildings; but buildings do not make a school. St. Paul's with its tiny classrooms, and toilets across the yard, no staffroom or store rooms, there was nevertheless a well-ordered programme, a very happy atmosphere, and a reputation for good academic results.

I left in November 1947 on the same day that Miss Fallows retired. In later years our son and daughter both attended the new school where the old traditions were continued and they too have very happy memories of their years there.

Peggy Hartley

CHAPTER 9
St. Paul's School 1947 - 1970

The Old to the New

My appointment as Headmaster was announced in the Church Magazine in August 1947.

"THE NEW HEADMASTER

The Managers have appointed Mr. Sidney Percival Bundy to succeed Miss Fallows, who relinquishes her office on 30th September 1947.

Mr. Bundy is a local man who received his training at the Church of England College in Chester and later taught in Wallasey. Since 1931 he has held appointments at various Barrow schools. He served in the Royal Navy from 1941 and has since been First Assistant at the Ocean Road School.

It will be seen that Mr. Bundy brings to his new office a wide experience which will stand him in good stead. He comes to us at a critical moment in the history of our School, which has served this neighbourhood for well over one hundred years. Now we are looking forward to the new School Building, for which the Church and Parish have for the last three years been raising funds.

The new Head inherits a great tradition, of which we are justly proud, and follows a succession of Head Teachers who have enabled St. Paul's School to play a leading role in the Educational System of the Borough. We give him a hearty welcome, both to his important office and to the fellowship of the Church, confident that under his leadership the School will maintain and enhance its deservedly high reputation and continue to advance the Christian cause in our Parish."

I commenced my duties on the 5th November 1947. The Vicar, the Revd. Norman Robinson, conducted Assembly and welcomed me on behalf of the School Managers. Also present, was Colonel Wilson, Chief Organiser, who brought good wishes from Mr. W.G. Bate, Chief Education Officer and Alderman F. Longstaffe, Chairman of the Education Committee. Unfortunately, Norman Robinson, the instigator of The School Building Fund Appeal, was about to leave the Parish. His knowledge of the facts concerning the decision of the School Managers and the Local Education Authority on the future status of the School, the termination of the Infant Department and the subsequent need for a catchment area to sustain the numbers on roll to keep the Junior Department viable, would have been invaluable, to all concerned in the early 1950s.

On the 17th December 1947, the Vicar received a farewell presentation from the scholars. Peter Simm gave the 'speech' and Vanessa Condon, the first child baptised by him as Vicar of St. Paul's, made the presentation.

After reading the notice of my appointment and listening to the welcome I received at this Assembly, I realised for the first time, what was expected of me and the challenge presented by my new role.

Firstly, this was to maintain the traditions and academic excellence set by my predecessors and a close relationship with the Church. Secondly, to prepare for the advantages offered by a new building in its own beautiful 'green' site, coupled with a fresh outlook on Primary Education as envisaged in the Education Act of 1944. The Local Education Authority had already inaugurated a system of annual tests in Arithmetic, English and Verbal Reasoning for all children of Junior age 7+ to 11+. The object of these tests was to enable the Headteacher and the Authority to examine a pupil's progress during their four Junior years, to provide remedial classes or groups for those whose attainment did not match their potential and to provide a system of selection for Secondary School Education at the completion of their Junior School Course. No longer would pupils be assessed on the results of a one day test.

My appointment as Head of the "new school" turned out to be merely a promise and not a reality. St. Paul's School opened on 26th September 1879 as a replacement for the first small school built on Abbey Road in 1843. This building, used for generations, both as a Day School, Sunday School and Parish Hall would probably have been replaced if war had not broken out in 1939. In 1941 it was badly damaged by enemy action but thoroughly repaired. During this period some lessons took place in the Church Vestry. Plans were then made to rebuild and an appeal was launched, by which over £5,000 was raised in three years. Think what that sum represents today! However, due to the building restrictions of the 1940s, under which other necessary projects received priority, no start could be made in planning, although the present site in the Paddock in the grounds of Drumard House, Hawcoat Lane, had already been reserved by the Local Education Authority.

The Closure of the Infant Department

The years 1948 - 1954, that is the first six years of my time as Headmaster, proved to be the most traumatic in the history of the school. Part of the agreement made by the Revd. Norman Robinson, the School Managers and the Local Education Authority was to change the status of the School from a Primary School of Infants and Juniors into a Junior School catering for children from 7 - 11 years. There were, at the time, very good reasons for this, but the statistical problems of gradually closing the Infant Department and the intake of sufficient children of Junior age to make the School viable had never been fully anticipated. I have attempted, by using extracts from the School Log Book, to demonstrate how the transition took place.

On 13th October 1948, the School Managers received this report on a General Inspection of the School in June 1948 by two of His Majesty's Inspectors:-

"In this School, there are 173 children of age range 5 to 11 years. They are organised in four Forms under a Headmaster and three Assistant Mistresses all of whom are qualified.

Of the four classrooms two are small, each having an area of about

425 square feet and they house large forms of 48 and 49 children. It is understood that arrangements have been made to reduce the numbers in these rooms from September 1948.

In spite of the existing cramped conditions gallant efforts are being made in the lowest Form to establish an atmosphere of freedom combined with purposeful activity. Here and elsewhere in the School good personal relationships have been established and valuable social training takes place.

The School has a long tradition of high standards of formal work and these standards are being maintained. Methods of teaching are, however, frequently less adventurous than they might be. It would be pleasant if the lighter touch which is used with the youngest children could percolate much farther up the School.

The Head Master, who was appointed in 1947, is sympathetic towards giving more play to the personal interests and creative abilities of the children, and he has already made moves in this direction. He has the support of a loyal and hardworking staff and he should feel encouraged to go forward. There are indications that the School may have an interesting period of growth ahead."

On the 15th May 1949, the Vicar the Revd. Arthur Briggs and the Chief Organiser visited the School to discuss with me the cramped conditions in the Infant Classrooms. It had been decided to reduce the number of Infants to be admitted in the previous Autumn Term. This was the first step towards the closure of the Infant Department. As a result of these discussions it was decided that Infants would no longer be admitted at the beginning of the Autumn Term 1953. This meant that the number of children on roll fell to 120, a loss of 53 children. This was an insufficient number to justify a staff of four teachers, based on the pupil-teacher ratio in force at that time. As a result, one teacher was transferred to another school and the School was reorganised into three classes. However, a fortnight later the decision was reversed and again the School was organised into four classes.

During part of this time I was absent from School, having undergone two eye operations. I will always be most grateful for the staunch cooperation of the staff and the sympathetic attitude of the School Managers and Mr. W.G. Bate, the Chief Education Officer. Under these circumstances parents and managers must have been worried about the progress in the School. In July 1952 the School was inspected again by H.M. Inspector Mr. Fuller. As a result I was assured by him that the standard of attainment had been maintained.

In July 1954, Miss Ella Martin and Miss Marjorie Helm retired after 35 years and 23 years loyal service to the school. The occasion was marked by a Social Evening. Mr. Harold Dunn, Secretary of the P.T.A. presented the two ladies with articles of furniture of their own choice. Miss Gertrude Fallows, Secretary of the School Managers presented illuminated addresses suitably framed. On the following day they received bouquets of flowers from the scholars.

This ended a long association with the School and severed the final link between the Infant and Junior Departments.

At the beginning of the Autumn Term, Miss J. Wallace joined the staff and the school was again reorganised into three classes.

In October 1954, H.M. Inspector Mr. Fuller who was taking a very active interest in the school, again paid a visit. On this occasion he was particularly interested in the high standard shown by the results of the Annual Entry Classification Tests. He asked if he could examine all class exercise books and reported that the results were a true reflection of the work done day by day in the classroom. He was most concerned that the school was, as stated, organised into three classes and as a result of his visit and with the cooperation of the Chief Education Officer and Chairman of the Education Committee a fourth teacher was appointed. These extracts from the Log Book show the situation:-

6.9.1955 School reopened for Autumn Term.

Miss I. Bradstock joined the school staff from St. George's Primary School and Miss E. Wilson from Training College. The children were classified into three classes.

8.9.1955

Mr. Fuller, H.M. Inspector visited the school at 3.30 p.m. He was concerned about the school organisation and hoped that a fourth teacher would be forthcoming. A Manager's meeting was held at 7.30 p.m. when an assurance was given that a fourth teacher would be available on the day that the school roll reached 130, the present roll being 127.

12.9.1955

Mr. Fuller, H.M. Inspector visited the school again and was assured that steps were being taken to qualify for the fourth teacher.

16.9.1955

Mr. Ruscoe, Chief Organiser visited the School as it appeared likely that the school roll would be increased to 130 on Monday 19th September. Arrangements were being made for a temporary appointment to be made early next week.

19.9.1955

The School Roll now 130. Mrs. J. Emmett visited the School and after careful consideration expressed a desire to be appointed as fourth teacher. With the cooperation of the L.E.A. and the Vicar, Mrs. Emmett was appointed to start work on the following day.

20.9.1955

Mrs. Emmett commenced duties. The School was reorganised into four classes with one age group per teacher.

On the 11th and 28th October 1955 Mr. Fuller inspected the school again and on the 5th March he discussed his highly satisfactory report with the School Managers. He continued his interest by addressing the P.T.A. on the 16th January 1956 on the topic "The Function of a Junior School". He retained his interest until the "New School" was established and paid his farewell visit on 23rd March 1961.

The Referendum and the Decision to

Build a New School

In 1955, St. Paul's Parochial Church Council decided to take action. A card referendum was taken on whether the building of a new school had the backing of the parishioners. As a result, a public meeting was held on 6th April 1955 to debate and consider the motion - "Before we cut the first sod - THINK! Count the cost. Discover the need. Consider - Is it the will of God?" The verdict was favourable and the School Appeal Fund was reopened.

Rev. E. J. Hay Hicks and St. Paul's Church Choir Boys
Open Air Service at Biggar Bank 1956

On the 25th April 1956 a joint meeting was held to formulate a plan of action. Among those attending were the Vicar, the Revd. E.J. Hay Hicks, School Managers, Mr. W.G. Bate Chief Education Officer, Mr. Fuller Her Majesty's Inspector and Architect Mr. Gerald Jackson. Plans for the new School acceptable to all parties were sketched. The next step forward took place in November 1956. This is an extract from the Parish Magazine:-

> *"Public Meeting*
> *Quite a good number turned out on 26th November, though the*
> *evening had been a soaker a little earlier. All who came were most*

*interested. The plans were cast on the screen by the kindness of Mr.
Yates. Canon Nurse took the chair very ably, the Vicar gave a review
of what had happened up to the present and then Mr. Renton described
the advantages of the new plans. Alderman Longstaffe explained how
the Local Education Authority were behind the scheme and the share
that they are already bearing. Mr. Bundy explained how advantageous
the new plans are from the teacher's point of view, and than an appeal
was made for widening the support. The Parent Teachers' Association
kindly provided refreshments."*

Sketch of the new school North Western Evening Mail November 30th 1956

Dedication of the Site

The first step forward was taken on the 25th February 1957 when the Right Reverend
Thomas Bloomer D.D. Lord Bishop of Carlisle dedicated the site. The ceremony was
recorded in the Church Magazine as follows:-

*"Yesterday was a very important occasion in the lives of the people
who live in St. Paul's Parish.*

It was the day of the dedication of the site of St. Paul's new school.

It was quite cold with rain occurring at intervals. At half past three parents and friends of the pupils began to arrive. Then at four o'clock a procession led by St. Paul's Scout band came on the scene. Behind the Scouts came the Cubs, then the Guides, the Brownies and last the children of the school.

At four fifteen the service started. First everyone sang "All people that on Earth do dwell". Then Alderman Longstaffe made a speech and in his speech he handed over the site of the new school to the Education Committee. Then the Vicar of St. Paul's, the Reverend E.J. Hay Hicks made a speech. The Bishop of Carlisle then followed the Vicar's speech.

When he had finished there were three prayers said and they were followed by the hymn, "Praise the Lord Ye Heavens adore Him." Then everyone marched back to school.

The children had an ice-cream each while the parents could go inside the school for a cup of tea. One room was reserved for the clergy and the important people. The Mayor of Barrow was at the ceremony and so was the Bishop of Penrith. Later, at about five o'clock when everyone was ready for coming home, it started to rain. All afternoon the weather had looked doubtful, but it kept fine all though the service."

Trustees and Managers under the Chairmanship of the Revd. E.J. Hay Hicks engaged Mr. F. Gerard Jackson as architect and Messrs. William Hull & Sons Ltd. to build the first part of the new School as authorised by the Ministry of Education. Work went apace and on Saturday 19th October 1957 the new £10,000 wing of St. Paul's School was officially opened by Mrs. Opher, wife of Mr. W.D. Opher, head of Vickers Armstrong (Barrow) Ltd.

Mrs. Opher was presented with an inscribed Prayer Book by the youngest pupil of the School, seven year old Jean Metcalf.

Fund raising went ahead and money came in from many sources including the sawing up, chopping up and selling of firewood, organised by Mr. Sam Price, Headmaster of the Boys' Grammar School, parent of past and present pupils and a good friend of the school. His wife Barbara, who was a member of the P.T.A. could be seen from Hawcoat Lane leading her team of choppers.

Extract from the Barrow Evening Mail:-

£130 raised at fete for school fund

"A sum approaching £130 was raised for St. Paul's Church School Building Fund by the fete organised by Dalton Deanery at the Strawberry Football Ground, Barrow on Saturday.

Attractions included a fancy dress competition, a baby show, a fencing display, pony rides and a variety of stalls, all parishes in the Deanery having contributed.

It was opened by Canon Norman Robinson, now at Penrith, who, as Vicar of St. Paul's launched the first appeal for funds in 1944.

"I can certainly say that there can be no occasion in the Parish of St. Paul's which could give me greater pleasure than one connected with the fund for your new school", he said. "I have been tremendously interested in it."

He recalled that the fund started 13 years ago with a gift day scheme that embraced thousands of people in hundreds of homes.

'A GREAT SCHOOL'

"Here we have a great school with a tradition going back over a century," and added Canon Robinson, "I pray that you will have every success in your efforts, and I wish you God speed and God bless."

Canon Robinson was introduced by the Rural Dean of Dalton, Canon C.E. Nurse, who pointed out that the school would serve the whole town. The Headmaster, Mr. S.P. Bundy, announced that the first part of the new school would open in September. Thanks to all who took part were expressed by Canon Nurse and by the Vicar of St. Paul's, the Rev. E.J. Hay Hicks."

Five little girls all dressed up for the fancy dress parade were (left to right) Jane Hodkinson, Sarah Croft, Pamela Quarrie, Deborah and Victoria Seddon. All were chosen first prize winners for the prettiest costumes.

For the next three years, the School met for Assembly in the old school building and then moved into classrooms in both buildings for lessons. Building permission was finally granted for the completion of the School, which was formally opened by Lord Knollys, Chairman of Vickers Ltd., on 30th September 1960. A plaque mounted in the School foyer and presented by the builder, Mr. Henry Hull, commemorates the occasion.

Here is an extract from "Vickers News.":-

> The official opening by Lord Knollys of the St. Paul's Church of England Junior School in Hawcoat Lane. This is the third building for this school, which has existed since 1843.
>
> The cost was £30,000, of which about a third was raised by the Church from contributions by the parishioners with help from the diocese and local industry, including Vickers-Armstrongs.
>
> Lord and Lady Knollys were welcomed by the Bishop of Carlisle, Dr. T. Bloomer, and the Chairman of the Barrow Education Committee, Alderman F. Longstaffe, the Vicar of Newbarns and Hawcoat, the Rev. A.R. Fountain, and the Headmaster, Mr. S.P. Bundy. The architect of the school Mr. F. Gerald Jackson, handed over the key.
>
> In his speech, Lord Knollys said that some technical and scientific education might be partly wasted unless pupils had a good junior foundation.
>
> He congratulated the people responsible for this 'great day' and said it was an event' that must bring particular satisfaction to Alderman Longstaffe because of the good work he had done for so long.
>
> Modern architecture, as in this school, contributed much to people's cheerfulness.
>
> He was particularly pleased to be there because his company thought that Barrow had a 'very outstanding type of community' and the company was proud to be connected with any community activity.
>
> In this area, there was a close link between industry and education. Industry had realised this need and responsibility, and had helped to this end for some time now.
>
> Lady Knollys then presented commemorative badges to the school's pupils and a bouquet was presented to her by Carol Wood, a pupil of the school.
>
> The fathers of many of the children work for the company and, after the ceremony, Lord and Lady Knollys had an opportunity to talk to the parents who were present.

A GOODLY HERITAGE...............

This is a facsimile of an essay written by a third-year pupil after the whole school had moved into the new building.

Carole Wood.   26. 4. 60.

Our New School

April 26th is the greatest day since
the two lower classes were built, As the
extension of St. Paul's C. of E. school
has been finished. It consists of two
very roomy classrooms, a very nice hall,
one office, one storeroom, I think it is, and
a very nice teachers room. The school is
not quite finished yet. The walls need
painting and a touch here and there and
it will be complete. It has been well
furnished with lovely new desks and chairs
and also new cupboards, wash basins,
toilets, clothes racks, lights and many other
things. We have lovely big classrooms with
very big windows. From one window you can
see Howcoat Lane, from another the back
of the Police Station, While the others look
out onto the playground.

The Start of a New Era

The official opening of the New School took place in 1960 but I recorded in the Log Book that the School was occupied after the Easter Holidays in April. This was a great relief to me because for the last three years I was Headmaster of the oldest school in Barrow and also part of the newest school. My main contact with the teachers and children in the New School was by a telephone link, school assemblies and a weekly visit. The number of children on roll was still low and steps were taken to attract the interest of more parents. The new building was used to host a meeting of St. Paul's Young Wives' Group and I spoke to them on "How can I Help my Child?" I was invited to speak to a similar Group connected with the Free churches. Mrs. Norah Seddon, a Foundation Manager, produced a pamphlet on behalf of the School Managers which was distributed as an inset to all Parish magazines in the Dalton Deanery.

On the 9th June 1961 a Manager's Meeting was held to examine the intake for September. This exceeded all expectations as 50 children of various ages between 7 and 11 years wished to be enrolled. This made it possible for a fourth teacher to be appointed and when the School opened for the Autumn Term, Mrs. K.R. Matthews joined the staff.

Progress in the School 1940 - 1970

While a lot of attention was being paid to the plans for building the new school, the fund raising efforts and the "fight to survive", the work and progress in the school continued.

In the late 1940's and the 1950s the school P.T.A. continued to meet, not merely as a fundraising body, with its mammoth jumble sales, but as a means of informing parents of progress in their children's school work and keeping them up-to-date with the changes envisaged in education as they became applicable. This was particularly useful when the Local Education Authority contemplated changing its plans for Secondary Education from the three-tiered system of Grammar, Technical and Modern Schools to the one-tiered system of Comprehensive Education.

These meetings were also a means of explaining to parents the introduction of "New Mathematics", the "Teaching of Oral French", and the possible introduction of "Sex Education" into the Junior School curriculum. One aspect of the Entry Classification Tests - the Verbal Reasoning Test was a difficult one to explain to parents and the Educational Psychologist was invited to talk and discuss this aspect of assessment of a child's ability.

A school uniform was introduced with a distinctive cap and blazer pocket badge designed by a former pupil indicating that the pupil was a member of a church school. Parents were always welcome to visit the school and a team of flower arrangers kept the entrance hall looking fresh and cheerful throughout the year. In the 1950s, the B.B.C. School Programmes were available through the installation of Rediffusion Radio Speakers in all classrooms. School trips with an educational bias were made

Class 4 1959, taken after the Annual St. Paul's School Leavers Service when each pupil was presented with an inscribed Bible. Standing L to R:- Mrs. R. Callister, Mrs. E. Williams, Rev. G. Lambert, Rev. Canon W. Bucks, Rev. H. C. Stewart, Rev. M. Nicklin, Miss I. Bradstock, Mr. S. P. Bundy.

each year, those to Malham Tarn, Chester, York, Ravenglass and Ingleton being of particular interest. Nativity plays, many written and composed by members of the staff, became an annual event. The School Leavers' Service and the presentation of a Bible to all Class Four leavers was also one of the highlights of the school year. In the 1960s, a portable television set was purchased by the P.T.A. and added interest was given to lessons, particularly to music lessons where singing and the playing of recorders, violins and other instruments were encouraged. Violin lessons, given after school hours by Miss Whitfield and later by Mr. Tony Drummond, attracted a number of young musicians. One of the most rewarding innovations was the teaching of Oral French. Here, both Staff and Pupils worked together with the help of Visual Aids, staff conversation sessions in the evening and the additional services of a part-time French teacher. We felt that the effort was worthwhile. The second innovation was the introduction of the "New Mathematics" Scheme, to herald, not only the approach of decimal coinage (new money) and the metric system of weights and measures, but a break away from "sums" to more thought provoking mathematics.

Physical Training, Swimming and Games took a more prominent part in the curriculum. Football and School Sports were played on the site of the New School until the L.E.A. provided a pitch at Clovelly Terrace. The girls played netball in the school yard, supervised by a class teacher and coached by volunteers, Mrs. Brenda Williams and later Mrs. Freda Webber. In the summer Term, through the kindness of Vickers' Sports Club and the cooperation of Mr. H. Nutton, whose two daughters were pupils of the school, a cricket pitch was provided and the Annual School Sports took place on Vickers' Sports Ground.

As more books became available, after the scarcity of the war years, the stock of teaching materials, library books, and topic books was built up. The teaching methods changed with the times but a sound grounding in English and mathematics was the basic aim. Formal teaching and group work went hand-in-hand.

Much could be written about the dedicated staff that a small school requires if it is to provide an all round education. I am most grateful to those who worked for and with me during the difficult times. They were:- Miss E. Martin, Miss M. Helm, Mrs. W. Parker, Mrs. D. King, Miss J. Wallace, Mr. W. Brough, Mr. A. Millardship, Mr. W. Marshall, Mrs. R. Callister, Mrs. H. Hepple, Mrs. M. Whitton, and especially Mrs. E. Williams (formerly Miss E. Wilson) who spent the whole of her teaching career at St. Paul's School. These dedicated teachers were followed by those who were responsible for building confidence when the new School was completed. They not only enhanced the reputation of the School but their work and ideas and the friendly atmosphere surrounded them fully justified all the "blood, sweat and tears" of the 1950s. They were:-

Mrs. E. Williams, Miss I. Bradstock, Mrs. K.R. Matthews, Mrs. M. Railton, Miss C. Gregg (later Mrs. C. Parnell). Also part-time French Teachers Mrs. O. Blacklock and Miss O. Davidson.

During the difficult times it was not all doom and gloom. We had some very happy times and our Class Christmas Parties were events which must have lingered in the minds of that generation. No discos - no rowdyism but good old-fashioned games, dances and competitions, ending with lovely teas, a true beginning for Christmas festivities. One year my participation in the festivities suffered a cruel blow. This was when the blackboard slipped off the easel, fell on to my left foot and broke my big toe. A deathly hush fell on the class and I still remember the sympathetic gasps from the children as I hobbled into Miss Helm's room for assistance. (Non-teaching personal friends thought it was a great joke, greeting it with hoots of laughter!).

I have only thankfulness and appreciation for the Clergy and School Managers. The Revd. Norman Robinson who started the School Building Fund Appeal, the Revd. E.J. Hay Hicks whose inspiration and determination resulted in the building being started. The Rev. Raymond Fountain and the Revd. Arthur Briggs who gave me such tremendous support.

All of these Ministers and their Curates made regular visits to the School, conducted an assembly and taught a class until 9.40 a.m. During Lent they cooperated in a series of lessons based on such topics as Famous Missionaries, the story of the East Window and the Apostles. We appreciated the assistance given by the Revd. John Hancock in adapting a new Diocesan syllabus of Religious Education to fit in with the syllabus provided by the Local Education Authortiy.

Diocesan Inspectors or Visitors arrived annually to conduct an examination of the Religious Instruction. These Ministers and their Curates took an active interest in the School. They visited the School frequently. Those who had children of their own were doubly interested in the progress and the happy atmosphere in the School. One H.M.

Inspector made a point of emphasising this happy spirit by commenting on the ethos of the School and the Revd. Arthur Briggs had this to say in the Church magazine of August 1948:-

"In my short time here, I have been very impressed by the tone and spirit of the School and by its intimate connection with the life and worship of the Church. This is, of course, as it ought to be, but it is good to realise it afresh and be thankful for all the School means to the Church and her children."

AN APPRECIATION

At the end of this current school term Mr. Bundy will have completed twenty-three years' service as Headmaster of St. Paul's Church of England Junior School and it is only fitting that we should place on record our appreciation of his work in our Parish.

Many families in this Parish and district owe a great debt of gratitude to Mr. Bundy for the education of their children, and the sound reputation of the School, built up over the years, is a fitting tribute to the Head and his staff.

On taking up his duties in 1947, the School was housed in the old school building then seventy years of age, and one cannot but feel that it was a "labour of love" to carry on, as he did for thirteen years, in an antiquated building which had only been given a new lease of life by the advent of war in 1939.

In 1960, Mr. Bundy had the satisfaction of seeing the present school completed with its up-to-date equipment and with a new incentive to move forward. The modern school stimulated interest, and applications for admission exceeded the capacity of intake, a condition which still prevails today.

The standard of education disseminated under Mr. Bundy's guidance, both in religious and secular instruction, is indeed very high and can best be judged by the excellent results which the school has achieved.

Under his guidance also, a very successful Parent-Teacher Association has operated which has proved of immense value to the working of the School.

At this point I would like to pay a personal tribute to Mr. Bundy whom I have known for more years than those covered by his Headmastership. About twenty years ago Mr. Bundy was elected as a Sidesman of St. Paul's Church which gave him great joy as thereby he was enabled to meet parents and children outside the environment of the school. In fact he very often assisted in Morning Service at Church by reading the lessons and for some time took part in a Children's Service once a month in church. His belief in the Christian Faith was never shaken. His devotion to the care and teaching of the children under his charge was of paramount importance and his fortitude in adversity, when he lost the sight of one eye, was phenomenal.

As a member of the Parochial Church Council, Mr. Bundy's advice was often called for and always readily forthcoming. We do thank him for this. He is now a valued member of the newly created Furness Deanery Synod and we trust that he will find enjoyment in serving on that important body.

He leaves the school to enjoy a well earned retirement and we would like him to know that he carries with him the very best wishes of his staff, the school managers, the members of the Parent Teachers' Association and the members of the Parochial Church Council, together with the parishioners generally, for a long and happy retirement, with abundant good health so that he and Mrs. Bundy can truly relax in enjoyment.

George Higham
Foundation Manager

The Editor of the Parish Post received this appreciation from Mrs. Rita Matthews as a result of the writer reading the articles on "Church and School" which were published in the Parish Post.

ST PAUL'S SCHOOL

A chance meeting with Mr. S. Bundy, the then Headmaster of St. Paul's Junior School, near Barrow railway station one day in 1961 led, for me, to eight of the happiest years of my teaching career. He mentioned that there was a vacancy at the school and I immediately offered myself as a possible candidate. I was at that time teaching in a local secondary school but wanted to broaden my experience, and, happily after an interview I began teaching with Mr. Bundy in September of that year. The school had only recently moved into the new building, and I was very impressed with the layout and organisation, and also the planning of the timetable. There was a full complement of 160 pupils - 40 children to a class, with 4 teachers, including the Head. Each classroom was self-contained and had its own facilities, but the staff were happy to leave doors open on occasions and we worked as a complete unit rather than as four separate entities. The children sat two to a desk facing the blackboard, something we rarely see nowadays, and I'm absolutely confident that they learned as much as they do today (if not more). The desks were often moved into a variety of positions for practical subjects, but a return to formality for written work gave the children a real sense of purpose.

Mr. Bundy consulted with all the staff on a regular basis, encouraging us to try experiments, make new plans, "do our own thing" and generally gave us free rein in the classroom while at the same time keeping a professional eye on us all. We taught from 9 a.m. to 4 p.m., with no free time, and certainly had no "inset days". The Head, of course, coped with all the administration of the school as well as carrying out full-time teaching.

The staff willingly undertook the teaching of French, when it was introduced into the junior curriculum, and we invited Mrs. Ottie Blacklock to refresh our memories, improve our pronunciation and correct our grammar, where faulty. We ran a weekly French class, when we practised the language and also discussed ways of making this new subject appeal to the children. I think we succeeded very well, although some time later, it was decided by the authorities that it was better to leave the learning of a second language until the secondary level.

We also entered into what was then called "New Maths" with great enthusiasm, had many and regular staff meetings to plan our projects, and spent hours of time after school making teaching aids. Our Art and Craft lessons (now known as C.D.T.) were organised in an informal way. The children had access to other classrooms to see what was happening, and we ensured that everyone benefitted from a number of different experiences each term.

All the lessons were a pleasure because the atmosphere in the whole of the school was conducive to learning. The children wanted to do well and also, I think, to please their teachers. We sought advice from the various local advisors (I think they enjoyed St. Paul's) and we listened to their opinions and ideas, but we always ensured that whatever they suggested would be beneficial to our children, rather than just accepting something because it was new or different. Visits from Inspectors, while not exactly welcomed, were an interesting occasion and I think we were all fairly confident that we were doing our best in educating the pupils.

Mr. Bundy was extremely keen on keeping tabs on every child's work and on our methods of teaching and so we knew that we were not going far wrong. We realised that these occasions were rather trying for the Head but the other three of us were not worried because we knew that he kept abreast of all educational innovations at that time and was genuinely concerned about each child.

Our day started with a religious assembly and I feel that this short period of coming together in quietness and respect made for a more gentle atmosphere and attitude in our school than I found in any other in which I taught. Behaviour was extremely good. Even in the playground we did not have any problems - the naughtiest boy I ever came across was chasing the girls with nettles!!

The children that I taught during my time at St. Paul's were all keen and interested, well-behaved and polite. Not, of course, all of the time, but we had no problems that really caused us any great anxiety. On the whole, the parents were very supportive, and not too critical, unless they were teachers and their child was not fulfilling their expectations! We had a very good P.T.A. at that time, whose members were really interested in education and, perhaps more importantly, remarkably efficient at fund-raising.

The mixed ability range in each class never presented a problem to any of the staff, and each child was encouraged to go as far as he or she could. It also ensured that they became tolerant of other children's strengths and weaknesses, accepted what they had to offer and were prepared to help their fellow pupils whenever they could. Homework was given on a regular basis if requested, or if a child was in need of extra help or practice in some subject. All classes had frequent table practice and spelling tests. I used to love them!

Our school trips were organised with meticulous care and great detail by Mr. Bundy, and the children always learnt something as well as having fun. Certainly there were no days out to Alton Towers!

Christmas was always a lovely time at St. Paul's. The Christmas play was a mammoth production, with all 160 children taking part. In spite of the fact that the staff became a little jaundiced during rehearsals, to see all of the children really believing in the wonderful story made it all worth-while. We also managed to fit in a concert or two from time, and I know that those who took part will remember the occasions with great fondness. I look back on my days at St. Paul's with great affection. I enjoyed the company of my fellow teachers, Eileen Williams and Ivy Bradstock, and benefitted from their advice and help. I do not think that there was a better Headteacher in Barrow at that time than Mr. Bundy, who was always willing to listen and encourage, and spared no personal effort in the service of his school.

Of course, my days there would not have been so happy without such wonderful pupils.

Mrs. Rita Matthews

Marjorie Gorry (nee Cooper) told Parish Post readers of her memories at St. Paul's as follows:-

Coat pegs and Snacks

I know now what it feels like to suffer from amnesia! When the Editors asked for my memories as an "old" pupil of St. Paul's School, I agreed. Little did I realise how difficult it was going to be to cast my mind back three decades!

The school was housed in what is now the Parish Hall. There were two infant and two junior classes. Miss Martin and Miss Helm were my infant teachers. My earliest memories are of the cloakroom pegs. As infants we used the two smaller rooms on the Hawcoat Lane side of the building, each having its own cloakroom and each peg having its own individual picture. I also remember, vividly, a pink metal tray upon which we placed our playtime snack. This usually consisted of a homemade biscuit, carefully wrapped in paper and with our names written on the little packet for easy identification. Snacks were eaten at playtime along with a bottle of milk (1/3 pint) drunk with a straw. We took it in turns to be milk monitors.

Mr. Bundy was our headmaster. He had charge of the older Juniors and commanded great respect as he does still! His hair style hasn't changed much! The Junior classes used the large hall with a partition to divide the space into two classrooms. This partition was moved back for certain events like Christmas Parties and Carol Services. I can still remember feeling scared when reading my part in a Christmas Service. It was Luke Chapter 2 verses 1-7 "And it came to pass in those days..."

In the junior classes we used double desks with tip-up seats and desk lids (some squeaked terribly). These desks contained ink-wells which needed filling regularly. We wrote with dip-in pens and had our weekly issue of pink blotting paper given out by the ink monitors.

Looking back, our school work was organised very formally. I think that gave us a feeling of security and order.

I still shudder at the mention of mental arithmetic. Eleven plus exams also sent shivers down our spines, as did the thick brown foolscap envelopes we had to take home containing our results - "Which Senior School am I going to?" was the cry.

As juniors, we looked forward to games and P.E. lessons. When we did country dancing, we had to move all the desks out of our classroom into the cloakroom to give us the necessary space. We were exhausted before we'd even danced one step of "Strip the Willow" or "The Eightsome Reel". Our present day school is built on what was our playing fields. The boys went to play football there. The pitch had a wonderful banking running across the centre line- it was an advantage to win the toss and play down slope first! Sports Day was held on these fields too. At some point, I remember using Vickers Sports Club indoor and outdoor facilities.

The Abbey Swimming Baths were in the process of being built, so swimming lessons didn't exist. Our present pupils are lucky enough to be be able to use Dalton Baths. Our junior girls were able to play netball - Miss Wilson taught us. The pitch ran alongside Hawcoat Lane and I think we took it in turns to graze some part of our anatomy along the sandstone walls during our netball lessons.

School visits were few and far between. They consisted of visits to Manor Farm in the springtime to see the new-born lambs and calves. We also had visits to Furness Abbey to tie in with our history lessons.

During our last year at school, about eight of us used to walk down Oxford Street on one afternoon each week clutching our violin cases. We had our violin lessons at Victoria Junior School. This one hour a week was regarded as real freedom and helped give us a feeling of independence.

The circle has gone full turn now and I am still involved with the school both as a part-time teacher and as a parent. Certain things remain as they were - which is rather comforting. We had maroon blazers, regular talks from the Vicar, services in church, just as our present pupils. We could even save our pocket money - not in the Savings Bank, but by buying 2/6d saving stamps from the school secretary.

At one time, I believe, the secretary worked at a desk behind the piano in Mr. Bundy's room. Later she was secreted away in what is now a store cupboard used by the Rendezvous group!

I hope our present pupils will remember their Primary school days as happily as I do. The facilities and resources provided now are certainly more sophisticated than we were lucky enough to have.

Marjorie Gorry

CHAPTER 10
St. Paul's School 1970 - 1989

Within a very short time after my resignation was received, the appointment of my successor was made. He was a young man, Hilary Riley, who was to prove, over the next nineteen years, to be an asset to the Church and the School. He was to maintain the close links between these two bodies, serve as a Leader in the Sunday School, a Sidesman, a member of the P.C.C. Deanery and Diocesan Synods and Churchwarden. His appointment was announced in the Church Magazine.

MR. H.J. RILEY - ST. PAUL'S SCHOOL'S NEW HEADMASTER

While we shall be sad to lose Mr. Bundy as Headmaster of St. Paul's Junior School, it does give us the opportunity of welcoming his successor. Mr. Riley comes to us with a varied experience in both teaching and administration. After leaving Keighley Boys' Grammar School, he was a Local Government Officer in the Education Department at Keighley. He was trained as a teacher at Sunderland Training College, and in 1961 was appointed Assistant Master at Ingrow County Primary Junior Mixed School, and he held a graded post from 1966. In 1968 Mr. Riley was appointed to his present post as Headmaster of Keelham County Primary School, a rural school with three teachers and 71 children. It is obvious that Mr. Riley is well qualified to succeed Mr. Bundy with this experience behind him, and also as he is already a headmaster.

But more than this, we shall be able to welcome the new headmaster into the congregation of St. Paul's as a man who takes an active part in the life of his Parish church. Since 1965 he has been churchwarden at St. Paul's Denholme, in the Diocese of Bradford, parish representative to the Ruri-Decanal Conference, and business manager of the Parish Magazine. In 1968, Mr. Riley directed a successful Stewardship Campaign, and for four years he has been a member of the Bradford Branch of the Telephone Samaritans.

Mr. Riley, his wife Sylvia, and their children, Lynne Susan, 7, and David Mark, 4 move into their new home on July 24th. We look forward to their joining us in worship, and we welcome them as partners in the all-embracing work of the Gospel of Jesus Christ.

In 1991 I asked Hilary Riley to contribute an article to the Parish Post on the development of St. Paul's School during his time as Headmaster. The following appeared in the August issue.

After two years as Headmaster of a village primary school in the West Riding of Yorkshire, I was privileged to take up my appointment as Headmaster at St. Paul's Church of England Junior School, Barrow in Furness in September 1970.

For the first few years I was a full-time teaching head and then in charge of a class for fifty percent of my time - sharing the actual teaching of Class 4 with my wife Sylvia. Happily our marriage and the school survived! Next, although having a teaching time-table, I was not in full-time charge of a class.

During most of these years I was also Churchwarden at St. Paul's and the school enjoyed close links with the Church. Many of the pupils will have happy memories of Revd. Frank Dean's assemblies and several of the older children fond memories of Pathfinder weekends, rambles up Coniston Old Man and other such activities.

On joining the school, Mrs. Williams, deputy headteacher, was invaluable in explaining the peculiarities of the Barrow educational scene. For example, in the Barrow Borough at that time it was a "closed shop". I was not allowed to apply for any headships in the Borough. In fact, the Aided sector was the only sector which allowed application from outside the Borough. The majority of my colleagues (who made me extremely welcome) had been at infant school, junior school, Barrow Grammar School, teacher training and then back as assistant teachers in the Borough and then headmasters.

Comprehensive education was due to commence in 1970 but in actual fact didn't start for several years. We operated selection to secondary schools with not just an eleven plus selection, but tests in each of the four junior years. Children left St. Paul's to go to either a Grammar School, Technical School or Secondary Modern School. I have fond memories of being in charge of Roose School for the day whilst the headmistress, Mrs. W. Lyons was in charge of St. Paul's for the day. We acted as invigilators so that justice could be seen to have been done whilst the pupils completed their "tests".

On the educational scene, due to Mrs. Ashworth, Mrs. Railton and Mrs. Taylor, children thoroughly enjoyed spoken French. Frequently we were congratulated on their ability by the secondary schools.

During this time group work was expanded, including Primary Science. St. Paul's was the first primary school in Barrow to adopt the Cambridge University Press School Mathematics Project based upon investigation and problem solving. We moved into and through the decimal age to the computer age. The computers were enjoyed and the expertise and enthusiasm of Mrs. Silcocks and other staff benefitted the children.

We were the first primary school in Barrow to invite parents to view their child's work on an appointment system and had a remarkable one hundred percent take up by the parents. We were also one of the first schools to involve parent helpers, on a "time and talents" scheme inside the classroom.

Countless parents, grandparents and relatives have been truly moved by our traditional Nativity plays. The true meaning of Christmas has been aptly conveyed, largely due to the dedication and skill of Mrs. Eileen Williams.

Musically, Mrs. Booth's instrumental groups, recorder and percussion groups, have been given skill and pleasure which have inspired many to take up an instrument in later life.

It is impossible to mention more than a glimpse of these nineteen years. Above all the happy memories of hikes, trips, sporting events, jumble sales, musical spectaculars, staff, governors, parents and last but most importantly, children are indelibly etched in my mind. What we tried to do was to provide a happy, caring, stable, Christian environment with high standards educationally, spiritually and morally.

Hundreds of children, now responsible well balanced adults, bear testimony to our success.

Hilary Riley

The result as you can see, is very revealing and shows that the school, staff and pupils have moved truly into the computer age, just as in my time they moved from very formal mathematics into the age of "new maths" as it was called. On the occasions when I visited the school, usually by the kind invitation of the Headteacher, I could see and sense that the St. Paul's tradition, or as one of Her Majesty's Inspector of Schools expressed it to me, "the ethos of the school" was very apparent. One of my most delightful visits occurred on the 25th Anniversary of the opening of the "new school". To mark this event, the older pupils had carried out a detailed study of the history of the school and the results of their work was on display. A birthday cake to commemorate the Anniversary was lit with candles which were extinguished in the traditional manner.

Birthday joy: Clair Cubiss left, and Laura Taggert, whose birthdays are tomorrow, get ready to blow out the birthday cake candles at celebrations to mark the 25th anniversary of St. Paul's Church of England School, Barrow. With them in the picture are present headmaster Mr. Hilary Riley and past head Mr. Sid Bundy

The Retirement of Hilary Riley

and Eileen Williams

The climax of Hilary Riley's career at St. Paul's coincided with the retirement of Eileen Williams who joined the school as a young teacher in 1955. Presentations to both Head Teacher and Deputy Head Teacher were made in church at the "Leavers Service" and I was honoured to take part in this memorable event.

Mrs. Freda Webber, whose close connections with the school began when her daughter, Gillian was a pupil and who was secretary to the School Governors for many years recorded the occasion in the Parish Magazine of August 1989.

The 19th July was the occasion of a joint celebration, the school leavers' service and the presentation to Mr. Hilary Riley (Headmaster) and Mrs. Eileen Williams (Deputy Head) on their retirement. A large congregation of Mums, a few Dads, Grand-parents and members of St. Paul's attended.

Mrs. Margaret Boummphrey, representing Revd. Canon Rex Chapman, held the children's attention with her interesting talk to them before presenting each Fourth Year pupil with an inscribed Bible.

A delightful rendering of variations on the well-known song Frère Jacques (arranged by Mrs. Booth) was played by sixteen boys and girls on recorders and glockenspiels.

Mr. S. Bundy, in his introductory speech to the presentation, reminded us how fortunate the school had been this century in that Mr. Helm, Mrs. Cooke, Miss Fallows, Mr. Bundy himself and Mr. Riley had all served for nineteen years or more giving a continuity which resulted in the excellent standard in the school. Mrs. Williams was presented with a cheque which she will use to purchase a painting and Mr. Riley was given binoculars, a Filofax Diary and a cheque.

Money collected from the school and congregation had been pooled.

Mr. G. Wilson on behalf of the church gave Mrs. Williams a bouquet of flowers and Mr. Riley a copy of the New International Version of the Bible.

Mrs. A. Woodall presented a book token to them both on behalf of the governors.

A very pleasant occasion was rounded-off with tea and orange squash served by members of the P.T.A. and many took their drink outside into the beautiful sunshine whilst some parents took photographs of the leavers with Mrs. Williams and Mr. Riley.

N.B. Mrs. Williams served the school for thirty four years and Mr. Riley for nineteen years.

Freda Webber

This is a young pupil's impression of his school when Mr. Riley was headmaster.

"My name is Jason. I am nine years old and I am a third year pupil at St. Paul's C. of E. School. My school is surrounded by trees and has a nice big playground. I spend a lot of time at school, sometimes I like it, especially on Thursdays when we go to the swimming baths and have art and bakery. On Wednesdays we have football. On Fridays, we work very hard all day, we learn lots of new things at school and sometimes we have homework to do."

Jason Mellors

So another chapter closed in the history of the school and with the advent of the new head teacher Mr. Richard Sanderson The parish is being kept informed of school projects and events through the newsy articles published from time to time in the Parish Post.

So another chapter closes.

CHAPTER 11
St. Paul's School 1989 - 1993

*"In last month's issue of the Parish Post (June 1989), the retirement
of the Head Teacher of St. Paul's School, Mr. Hilary Riley and the
Deputy Headteacher, Mrs. Eileen Williams was announced. We are now
happy to announce that appointments have been made to fill both of these
vacancies. The new Head Teacher is to be Mr. Richard Sanderson, at
present Head of Langdale Church of England Primary School. The new
Deputy Head teacher is to be Miss. Jacqueline Dowie".*

Mr. Richard Sanderson has now completed three years as headmaster. His monthly
articles in the Parish Post have been much appreciated and have kept us informed of
the activities and exciting experiences enjoyed by the pupils. It has been a period of
change and in asking him to give me some impressions of these changes I have
appreciated more than ever the problems of administrating the many and often, lengthy
and intricate instructions raised by "The Department" or `The Ministry' (of Education
(- not the Rector!))

The Latest Era

I took over the headship from Hilary Riley in September 1989. This, as the title
suggests, coincided with the start of a whole series of massive changes in education,
which were included in the legislation known as the Education Reform Act (E.R.A.).
I was fortunate because I was already a Head in Cumbria, therefore familiar with the
role of headteacher and aware of the new legislation due to unfold. I also knew the area
and was fairly well acquainted with many of my colleagues who made me feel very
welcome.

Education was due to have an incredible amount of change imposed upon it by this
new government legislation. These changes have been immense, and there are still
some yet to come into force. The huge upheaval will be felt by everyone involved in
education for the next fifteen years.

I am tempted to give you details of these changes and their effects, but realise for
many this would not be riveting reading! Perhaps by briefly explaining some of the
major ones, I can give you an insight into what this has meant for schools.

Probably the most obvious change is the Local Management of Schools (L.M.S.)
which effectively gives the headteacher and governors a greater amount of control over
aspects of school which were previously organised by the L.E.A. The result is far more
work for the headteacher and governors, particularly the amount they have to
understand and the number of sub-committees on which they need to be. Schools are
now formula funded, which means greater financial control. This tends to lead to
frustration, particularly because of the inadequacy of funding for the primary sector
and junior schools specifically. Budgets and expenditure also have to be carefully

prepared and monitored.

At exactly the same time as the above changes, the National Curriculum was introduced. This, during the last three years, has developed to include nine subjects, along with Standard Assessment Tasks (S.A.T.S.). Of the other changes, perhaps the next most significant has been the privatisation and separation of all the services on which schools rely, e.g school dinners, grounds maintenance, supplies etc. They are no longer automatic and relationships established over many years have totally changed or vanished.

As a headteacher, both before and after E.R.A. it is interesting to reflect on some of these changes and the great pressure they have exerted in terms of administration, organisation and extra work on schools like St. Paul's. However, despite all these ongoing changes, we have not been diverted from the prime purpose of our school, which is education. The very professional staff at St. Paul's have continued to maintain very high standards.

Having reflected on the aspects of change over which we have no control, but where possible we have used positively for the benefit of our school, I would like to look at some recent developments that we have generated.

Charged with the responsibility of delivering the National Curriculum, we have taken the opportunity to review all aspects of the school curriculum. We have worked together using the considerable talents and professionalism of all members of staff. In this way, we have built on the sound base which existed at St. Paul's to widen the curriculum to include all subjects as appropriate.

Our curriculum has breadth, depth, relevance and provides the children with exciting and stimulating learning opportunities. One feature incorporated are class assemblies which are a part of the work being done by the children. We have also incorporated regular educational visits into the work being done by the children. These can be anything from a visit to the old school, or a day at the museum of science and industry in Manchester. In fact the children in the last three years have benefitted from a long list of various locations. A child's comment from a recent visit studying woodland industries on Haverthwaite Heights springs to mind: 'It's great, just like exploring a jungle'.

Two special developments that have been very valuable educationally and extremely exciting are the Arts Workshop and the residential field visits. The Arts Workshops have been written by the children in small groups and then the completed production has been put together and shared with audiences which include friends, family, parents and recently children from our feeder infant schools. All the children have a part and therefore an opportunity to sing, act, dance and dress up. The residential visits have been for the oldest class (now called Year Six). They have experienced outdoor and environmental education, plus importantly an opportunity to develop independence by looking after themselves, which includes washing up and cooking!

We have also developed the partnership with parents, because we believe that working closely with parents is the best way to help the individual child. This has been done in a variety of ways which includes having a very active P.T.A. running a number of social and fund raising functions. Parents help in school in many different ways and we have termly parents meetings which are always extremely well supported.

Our children are very capable and we have involved them in many aspects of school life. Our bookshop which we started just over two years ago is run by the children. They organise games for some P.T.A. functions and act as monitors for many different aspects of school life. The children now have their own records of achievement and the whole philosophy of building on their own achievements is reflected in classroom teaching and in specific activities like the weekly achievement assembly.

Presentation to the Gemma Wood Appeal

I have enjoyed my three years at St. Paul's working with so many interesting children and a very professional staff. As an aided school we have a Christian philosophy which underlies all we do and means Christian values are as important to us as pure academic success. Our special relationship with the church is an important part of school life. We also consider ourselves a community school and are pleased to be able to help local groups, particularly St. Paul's uniformed organisations.

To finish this chapter in St. Paul's school history, I would like to look forward. At this moment the governors are actively involved in a campaign to have the school extended to include infants i.e. once again to become a full primary school. Wouldn't it be tremendous if, as part of our celebrations of 150 years as a school, we could announce that we had been granted permission to become a full primary school again.

Richard R.W. Sanderson

IN CONCLUSION.............

I have spent so much time reading and re-reading copies of the Church Magazines, kept as a record of the Church's history, that I feel that I have been part of that story. Certainly the social and spiritual life of the parish were closely knit, especially during the Ministry of the Revd. William Taylor. I grew up in a similar atmosphere in the Parish of St. Mary's, Walney. One reads of American Teas at the Vicarage; the Tennis Club, the Young Men's Debating Society; the Sewing Guild; the Life of the Scout and Guide Movement; the Girls' Friendly Society; Miss Phyllis Bell's Entertainment; the Rustic Concert Party led by Len Hardy and Eric Gaudie, (stalwarts of the Barrow Amateur Operative Society who gave their performances at the Royalty Theatre in Cavendish Street); The Palestine Exhibition of 1924 - the list seems endless. All of these events are reported in a spirit of enthusiasm, showing them to be enjoyed by all.

One other noticeable feature has been the beautifully composed obituaries recording the life and service both of the personalities of the Parish and the more humble and self-effacing worshippers.

In January 1922, a new topic was the subject of the Vicar's letter, namely the abolition of Pew Rents and the introduction of the Free Will Offering Scheme. During the next nine months much time and effort was given to the explanation of such a scheme and eventually in the September Issue of the Magazine this announcement was made.

> *"It will be remembered that the end of September marks the close of the custom of paying for sittings in church. Beginning with October, all seats in future will be free and we hope that all those persons whom we are told have stayed away from St. Paul's on account of pew rents will take note that their objection no longer holds good and we hope that they will find their way to their Parish Church where we shall be glad to welcome them."*

Seventy years have passed since the introduction of this scheme, now reinforced by the Covenant Scheme, whereby Income Tax already paid by the donor is reclaimed by the Church Treasurer and becomes a significant part of the Church's income at no cost to the donor.

As mentioned in an earlier article, School Fees, be they ever so small, were needed to maintain the building. They were abolished many years ago and the School Managers set up a School Subscription Scheme whereby Parishioners were encouraged to promise a definite amount over a period of five years. A pupil in 1985 had this to say about school fees:-

> *"In the Log Book it says that Infants had to pay two old pennies and children in Classes 1 to 6 had to pay five old pennies a week".*

Another source gives this explanation of the School Fees:-

> *"In the early days of St. Paul's School charges were 2 pence a week for reading, 3 pence for reading and writing, and 6 pence for these two subjects plus English grammar, geography and arithmetic".*

After the completion of the New School in 1960, sufficient money remained to enable the School Managers (now School Governors) to carry out their obligations from the interest accrued. The income cannot be used to supplement allowances received from the Education Authority for the purchase of books and materials. Today there is a need for more financial support and the P.T.A., started in the 1930s as a channel to stimulate parent involvement in school affairs, has taken on the principal role in raising these extra funds.

What does the future hold?

The Church - i.e. the Building - with its recent alterations and improvements should be "off the agenda" for the immediate future.

The Church - i.e. the People - now has time to take a serious look at its role in the Decade of Evangelism.

The School - i.e. the Governors - are very much occupied in dealing with the amount of paperwork that L.M.S. (Local Management of Schools) has brought about. They have also made a further approach to the Education Authority in their efforts to re-establish an Infant Department.

The School - i.e. the Headteacher, Staff and Parents - has the opportunity to provide the best academic training for the pupils. St. Paul's is a Church of England Voluntary Aided School. Its history shows clearly the desire that academic achievement and religious training should co-exist.

In 1955, when the Rev. E.J. Hay-Hicks launched the Church's campaign to build the New School, a pamphlet was sent to every household in the parish. One section dealt with the "Reasons for a Voluntary Church School" and I quote:-

RELIGIOUS

"We feel the need to stress religion as a first and fundamental principle in true education. In engaging teachers we look for those with a sense of vocation by God, and a strong desire to see first His Kingdom. It is our great wish to work harmoniously with the State system, and we rejoice that in many County Schools also there are teachers of a strong Christian convinction, but we go further - we believe that a simple and sincere faith should be emphasised before all else. This fundamental emphasis on religion has enhanced rather than impaired success and we are justly proud of recent results.

GEOGRAPHICAL

"This area is a widely scattered residential district with outlying farms. Parents of all Protestant Churches have, in the past, greatly appreciated the Church School. It has also proved a centre round which the scattered community has been a little more drawn together. This has been especially evident in the use made of the buildings after School hours.

These reasons are still valid.
The need is still there.
The link between Church and School is a precious one.

It is up to the present generation of Clergy and Teachers, Parents and Parishioners, Governors and the Parochial Church Council to strengthen the ties.

Sid Bundy

APPENDICES

"The Rewards of a Church School -

Educating the Whole Child"

Many well wishers did their best in bringing the needs of St. Paul's School before the parents in the parish. We were fortunate to have as a Foundation Manager, Mrs. Norah Seddon, wife of Dr. J. Seddon, whose six children attended the school as and when they reached Junior School age. On the 13th August 1959, one of her articles was published in the Manchester Guardian under the heading

Although St. Paul's School is not named, it was obvious that her observations were directly connected with her experience in Barrow.

It is interesting to note that one of her daughters is the talented feature writer for the Barrow Evening News - Deborah Kermonde

The passage of the Government's Education Bill, which received the royal assent on July 29 brought out the big guns of those who are afraid of the influence church schools may wield.

Stray bullets have been flying about, some of them shot off by people who castigate these schools for things they do not do, and indeed are not permitted to do under the 1944 Education Act.

When the smoke has cleared a little the Church of England's 3,500 or so Aided schools will still be found, getting on with renewed vigour with their job of educating, in co-operation with State and local authority, the whole child. Perhaps an account of the work of a particular Church school may blow a little cool air on to the subject. The school in question is a Church of England Aided Junior School in the North-west, and I write as a partisan - a foundation manager, and a parent, too.

Special experience

The running of Church schools today is a partnership between Church, State, and Local Education Authority. On our managing body the Church supplies four of the members and the Local Education Authority two - and this two-thirds one-third relationship is the same for all the schools affected by the Government's new measure. In our case, the four foundation managers are the vicar, the vicar's warden, myself, and a member of the Parochial Church Council whose special experience in building matters is invaluable to us. The Local Education Authority members (one from "each side of the house") are the chairman of the education committee - incidentally a Salvationist, and a manager for fifteen years - and a councillor with a child at our school. Also, ex-officio and without a vote, we have parents of former pupils as manager's treasurer and secretary. The head teacher attends all our meetings: he has no vote, but is a valued contributor in our discussions.

As school managers we appoint the teachers, although the Local Education Authority can reject any appointment we make if they are not satisfied with that teacher's professional merits. We choose our teachers with care and with prayer: a teacher is no less a teacher because he is a churchman, and we want the best teachers we can get.

The secular teaching in our school is under the control of the Local Education Authority, and is inspected by Her Majesty's Inspector in the same way as that of the local county schools.

According to some of our detractors, religious teaching at denominational schools is rammed down the children's throats at every lesson. There is truth behind this exaggeration. Certainly a child will absorb, unconsciously, the outlook on life of those who teach him. This outlook - that the God who invented mathematics and chemistry is still interested in these and other subjects - must be basic in Church schools, and perhaps is one of their most valuable contributions to education. Equally important is the link-up between religious teaching in school and the worshipping community - a link which the county schools, non-denominational in character, are unable to force.

In our school, religious teaching follows this pattern; there are a total of five religious instruction periods a week, during two of which the Agreed Syllabus of Religious Instruction for this area (drawn up by a local committee of Church of England clergy, Free Church ministers, teachers, and Local Education Authority members) is used as the basis of Old and New Testament teaching. In this way, when a child leaves our school for a county secondary school there is continuity of teaching. The religious instruction lessons also include hymn practice, listening to B.B.C. religious broadcasts for schools and activity methods in which the younger children express in picture, story, or play, the meaning of what they have learned.

A diocesan supplement to the agreed syllabus is used for two lessons for the older children, and one for the younger ones. This includes teaching about the Prayer Book services, the sacraments and the catechism; about baptism and confirmation; and about our parish church, its history, and its furnishings -the font, the Lord's Table, and so on. This teaching is linked up with the Bible, the life of our Lord, and the services used in Church. It is given by our head teacher or by one of the clergy.

School and Church are also linked by school services on special occasions, such as Harvest Thanksgiving, Education Sunday, and our patron saint's day. There is a weekly school service in Lent, and two of our happiest occasions are the Christmas Nativity play and the "Leavers' Service", when we give an illustrated Bible to each 11-year old leaving us for secondary education.

In Two Halves

At the moment our school is in two halves, an old building and part of a new one. We started to raise money for a new building about twelve years ago; the old school building dated from 1877, and 170 children, ranging in age from 5 to 11, were being taught in four classrooms. In spite of this desperate overcrowding, our school had a wonderful reputation and there was usually a waiting list for entry.

After reorganisation we stopped taking infants and gradually became a 160-place junior school. This eased the accommodation problem, but we still needed a new building; we had no separate hall, and playground space was inadequate. The building fund had raised £5,000, mainly through a penny-a-week collection, but when permission to build two classrooms of our new school was granted in 1957 we had to go into the finances of the whole thing pretty thoroughly. If we started building we would have to find for the complete new school about £15,000 - 50 percent of the total cost. Even with some diocesan help and an interest-free loan, this was a heavy load for a parish to carry.

The whole parish was therefore circularised and our people were asked to promise donations over a period of years. The response was sufficient, the money was promised, and we went ahead. Completion of our school is under way now. Whether the Government's new 75 percent grant will relieve us of any part of our burden, assumed before the new Act, is not yet clear, but whatever the outcome, our parish is committed to finishing this job.

Our school is a good school. We have no truancy, attendance figures are amazingly high - the children will not stay away without good reason - and there is the happiest relationship between parents, teachers, staff and children.

We are a one-class entry school and have no "streaming". Work is done within the classes in little groups and a child who improves can rise to the top without changing his teacher or his classmates. Examination results are first-class, but perhaps more important than these are the results we get with little "non-readers", with the awkward, shy, backward, harassed, or timid child. This is a school where every child has his place in the sun.

The three subjects - Faculties, Patronage and Simeon Trust - are familiar to members of the Parochial Church Council but other members of the congregation may have little knowledge of this. Hence their inclusion in the Appendix.

FACULTIES

The consecrated buildings and lands situated within a diocese are in the ultimate guardianship of the Bishop, who exercises his authority in this respect through his Chancellor. In consequence the legal procedure known as the application for and the granting of a faculty is necessary for the sanction of alterations in a consecrated building or its contents, or in a churchyard or other consecrated burial ground or its contents.

The faculty jurisdiction extends to unconsecrated land which forms, or is part of, the curtilage of a consecrated church. And it may also be extended, by an order of the Bishop, and during the period specified in such order, to any unconsecrated building which he has licensed for public worship.

The petition for a faculty is lodged in the consistory court of the diocese, before the chancellor as judge of that court. It is usually made in the name of the incumbent and churchwardens, but this is not necessary, since any person who is regarded by the law as having an interest is entitled either to apply for or to oppose the grant of a faculty; and for this purpose all the following persons are regarded as having an interest, viz. the parishioners, persons who though not resident in the parish are on its electoral roll, and the archdeacon; and also in some types of cases, certain other persons as well.

The object of obtaining a faculty is to ensure that the work proposed to be done shall not subsequently be interfered with, for if anything is done without the grant of a faculty, it is open to any parishioner, or other person having an interest, to apply for a faculty authorising the removal of the work. In such a case the incumbent and churchwardens, or any other person or persons also having an interest, may lodge a cross-petition for a confirmatory faculty authorising retrospectively what is sought to be removed.

Trivial additions to the church or its furniture, e.g. almsboxes or hassocks, do not require a faculty.

As regards the churchyard, no faculty is necessary for the burial of a body; on the other hand, a body cannot be removed from consecrated ground for burial elsewhere without a faculty. For the erection of a monument, a faculty is required in strict law, but usually this is not insisted on in practice, and the incumbent's approval is regarded as sufficient. If he refuses approval, the person desirous of erecting the monument can petition for a faculty to reverse his decision.

Trivial repairs or replacements do not require a faculty. But the decision whether a faculty is necessary in any given case rests with the chancellor, and it is desirable that any question of doubt should be referred to him.

No faculty may be granted for anything illegal, e.g. because it has a superstitious purpose, or because it would be inconsistent with the sacred purposes for which the building or land was consecrated. But within the limits of legality, the consistory court has an extremely wide discretion to give or refuse a faculty for almost any sort of work or innovation. This discretion must, however, be exercised judicially and for proper reasons. Certain considerations and restrictions are imposed by the Faculty Jurisdiction Measure 1964 on the grant of a faculty for the demolition or partial demolition of a church.

The jurisdiction of the consistory court extends only to those places where the Bishop is the ordinary. He is the ordinary for most of the geographical area covered by the diocese, but not for places known as peculiars, for example, Westminster Abbey, nor usually (and perhaps surprisingly) for his cathedral church where in most cases the dean (or provost) is the ordinary and sometimes the dean (or provost) and chapter fulfil that role. With such places, usually non-parochial, this book is not concerned.

There is in every diocese an Advisory Committee whose function it is to assist the chancellor on the one hand and the parishioners on the other. These committees usually consist of experts in architecture, archaeology, and art, who know the diocese and its churches. They are ready to advise the parishioners before the proposals are embodied in a petition for a faculty, and the chancellor on any proposals submitted to him. The advisory committee system has justified itself by results, and considerable attention is given to the committees by most chancellors. A Council for Places of Worship also exists, the purpose of which is to co-ordinate the work of the diocesan committees and to advise in cases which present special difficulty.

In a simple case, where there is no opposition, a chancellor may, and commonly does, grant a faculty without a hearing in court. But if in his opinion the case involves some legal or other difficulty or complication, he is likely to direct a hearing in open court; and he will always do so if the petition is opposed.

Under the Faculty Jurisdiction Measure 1964, Section 12, the archdeacon is empowered to issue a certificate for certain types of work which will take effect in lieu of a faculty, provided that application is made to him by the incumbent and churchwardens of the parish, and is supported by a resolution of the parochial church council, and is unopposed. The works in question are:

(a) Repairs to a church not involving substantial change in its structure nor affecting its appearance;

(b) Repairs to the contents of a church not materially affecting their nature or appearance;

(c) Redecoration of a church or its contents;

(d) Any alteration in an existing heating system not involving a substantial change in the church's appearance.

The chancellor may direct the same procedure with regard to any other application which, in his opinion, is unlikely to give rise to any controversy or dissatisfaction in the parish and is not important enough to justify the expense of faculty proceedings.

NEWBARNS VILLAGE

In an idle moment, perhaps sitting at ease by my fire, I catch the past and take a leap into childhood, when I lived in Newbarns Village in the 1920s and '30s. Of course there are changes now which it might be interesting to record. For instance, the busy thoroughfare of Hollow Lane was then a narrow lane with a hedge on one side and tall trees behind a high wall on the other. Behind the hedge there was a lovely hayfield with a little beck running the length of it, with a grand haystack built in the corner.

At the bottom of the hill stood "The Farmer's Arms", which again has been modified over the years. There was (and still is) a terrace of small houses which was added to in 1914 and then completed in the early '20s. Some of these, and others up Hollow Lane, were demolished in air raids but were rebuilt after the War.

There was a small shop, converted from two cottages, next to the Farmer's Arms, whose entrance was on the same line. The shop was exactly as one imagined it would be. It sold almost everything. Fresh bread (4½d old money), vinegar in a cask, and yeast in a hessian cloth, etc. The shop stood almost opposite the beautiful house at the bottom of Fairfield Lane, which only had houses on one side then. Next to this house, stood two houses with very long gardens, and then there was a barn that housed carts and horses. Taxis were not so common those days.

Hector Street faced the barn and had a little shop on the corner. Round to the right there was the heart of this little village with some small houses, now lovingly cherished, the little beck sees the light here; this is where the earliest celandines greeted the cold March days. Here we circle Sandylands Farm which is very old, and skirt Malvern House which is a landmark in the village.

There was another farm called Yew Tree that was the home of the Atkinson family. There used to be a lot of children playing about. There was a lamp post where they gathered to play skipping in the dusk and where anxious mothers came to get them in. It wasn't encouraged to stay out. This was by Yew Tree Hall which was privately owned by Mr. and Mrs. Mansfield. It was a very useful building and used for every purpose. There were whist drives, dancing classes, meetings at Christmas, and most exciting fancy dress balls attended by all the children in the village and lots of mums and dads as well.

As we leave this behind we go down Muddimans Lane which is now Lesh Lane. There was a little dwelling down here made from a railway coach - it made a cosy if somewhat unconventional home. Mr. Muddiman had some greenhouses and some fields for tomatoes and vegetables. They were lovely - freshly picked for each customer.

Passing from here down through two more fields - it was fields all the way from the village, no houses, only one could take the cinder path to the newly completed Abbotsmead Estate, and back to Newbarns via Cook Lane, now Friars Lane and Flass Lane to Harrel Lane and home.

Of course there was no Beacon Hill until the '30s, but the roads were good. It was a happy place to live. I still think it maintains many of its old qualities of neighbourly friendships, and remains a very happy environment in which to live.

Mrs. Clarice Rozze
nee Gillbanks), 84 Hollow Lane

PATRONAGE BOARD

When a vacancy occurs in the Parish of St. Paul's, Newbarns and Hawcoat, the Parochial Church Council receives this notice from the Bishop of Carlisle.

B.E.R.P. 2

Benefices (Exercise of Rights of Presentation) Measure, 1931

NOTIFICATION BY THE BISHOP TO THE PAROCHIAL CHURCH COUNCIL UNDER SECTION 1 OF THE MEASURE, WHEN THE BISHOP IS NOT THE PATRON

To the Parochial Church Council

of the Parish of. St. Paul Newbarns and Hawcoat

in the Diocese of. Carlisle

In pursuance of Section 1 of the above Measure, I am

directed by the Bishop of Carlisle to notify to you

that the Benefice of St. Paul Newbarns and Hawcoat (will shortly)

(has　　)

become vacant by the　(death　　)　of the Reverend ....
(cession　　)
(resignation)

The Patron of the Benefice is the Patronage Board constituted by a Scheme of the Church Commissioners which was confirmed by an Order in Council of....date.......

Dated...............Registrar........................... Bishop's Secretary

Address ....

SCHEDULE TO THE SCHEME

CONSTITUTION TO THE PATRONAGE BOARD

The patronage board referred to in clause 3 of this Scheme shall consist of:-

1. the following in right of their respective offices:-

(a) the Bishop, who shall be chairman of the board, and shall have one vote as a member of the board, and a casting vote as chairman;

(b) the archdeacon of the archdeaconry to which the benefice shall for the time being belong, who shall have one vote;

(c) one representivate of the parochial church council of the parish of Newbarns and Hawcoat, appointed from time to time by the said council, who shall have one vote.

2. three representatives of Simeon's Trustees, whose registered office is at 1, Selwyn Gardens, Cambridge, CB3 9AX, appointed from time to time by the said trustees, each of whom shall have one vote.

THE SIMEON TRUST

Charles Simeon (1759 - 1836) Leader of the Evangelical Revival. He was educated at Eton and King's College, Cambridge, where he became a Fellow in 1782. In 1783 he was ordained priest, and in the same year was appointed Vicar of Holy Trinity, Cambridge, holding this incumbency till his death. At an early date he had come under the influence of the two Venns and his whole future ministry was strongly coloured by his Evangelical experience. At first he was met by hostility both in the university and among his congregation, but his pastoral zeal broke down all opposition. He became a leading figure in the Missionary Movement, being one of the founders of the C.M.S. (1799) and a prominent supporter of the British and Foreign Bible Society; and he was frequently consulted by the East India Company on the choice of their chaplains. He was also the founder of a body of trustees (the Simeon Trustees) for securing and administering Church patronage in accordance with his principles.

Patronage

Horace Hayhurst in his booklet on St. Paul's Church records how Charles Simeon set up the Simeon Trust in 1833. This extract is taken from his booklet.

"Simeon realised that the question of patronage was important. Opportunities for serious and godly men being appointed to suitable livings were scarce. Simeon resolved to work for its improvement and reform. In the days when the purchase of livings was common practice, he felt justified in buying advowsons in order to ensure continuity of faithful ministry: 'others purchase income' he wrote, 'I purchase spheres wherein the prosperity of the Established Church and the Kingdom of our Lord may be advanced'. With money inherited from his brother, he continued to buy patronage and in 1833 founded the Trust which bears his name."

There are few references to the Simeon Trust in the Church Magazines.

When the Rev. A.R. Fountain was transferred to Faringdon, the Church Wardens reported on a meeting held with a member of the Trustees who was considering the matter of the appointment of his successor. Later in the year, George Higham, Vice Chairman of the Parochial Church Council stated that several clergymen recommended by the Simeon Trustees had visited the Parish but so far none had accepted the living. The Trustees persevered and eventually the Rev. Frank Dean was appointed. St. Paul's Magazine also reports that one of the Trustees was the Rev. Christopher Chavasse.

John Hodkin at my request, has researched the history of this remarkable man who was the incumbent of St. George's Church, Barrow in Furness from 1919 - 1922:- Christopher Chavasse, a Gallant Bishop

Christopher Chavasse, a Gallant Bishop

Of all the hundreds of clergymen who have served in Barrow over the past 70 years few, if any, went on to achieve greater distinction than Christopher Chavasse, Bishop of Rochester for twenty years.

He was a leading evangelical, but not a blinkered one, opposing as he did extreme conservative fundamentalism.

Chavasse was born in 1884, the eldest (and twin) son of the Rev. Francis James Chavasse then a Rector in Oxford, who became Bishop of Liverpool.

Chavasse was a distinguished athlete at Oxford University, gaining blue for lacrosse and athletics. Both he and his twin brother Noel, who was killed in the 1914-18 war, represented England in the Olympic Games of 1908.

After a curacy at St. Helens, Chavasse enlisted as a chaplain in the forces in 1914, and was awarded the MC and Croix de Guerre. He was promoted Deputy Assistant Chaplain General in IX Corps in 1918.

On being demobbed in 1919, he became Vicar of St. George's, Barrow. Someone who remembers him well describes him as being a man one could definitely look up to.

Chavasse left Barrow in 1922 and returned to Oxford where he played a leading part in the establishment of a new and evangelical college which aimed at attracting men of modest means and providing bursaries for ordinands.

In 1939 he was nominated to the See of Rochester, but his consecration had to be delayed until the following year owing to a boating accident in which he lost the use of a leg which had to be amputated.

He did much great work as bishop, despite his grievous handicap.

In 1944 he launched an appeal for a million pounds for rebuilding and augmentation.
He later launched a church extension campaign to provide churches in the new housing estates arising from the overspill of London's population.

His last years saw the creation of a third archdeaconry at Bromley and the suffragan bishopric at Tonbridge (a post held by our previous Bishop David Halsey before coming to Carlisle) and a diocesan centre at Chislehurst.

He also founded a theological college for older men at Rochester.

Chavasse, who was married with five children was a prolific author. In 1936, he produced "Charles Simeon; an Interpretation".

He retired in 1960 and died two years later aged 77.

JOHN HODKIN

The Barrow Blitz - Its effect on Church, Vicarage and School

The town of Barrow in Furness with its Shipyard and Steelworks concentrated on the western edge of the town seemed to be a prime target for enemy aircraft.

The A.R.P. Services were prepared for action in September 1939, but their response to action was not thoroughly tested until the dark nights of 1941. Part of this preparation was the formation of teams of fire-watchers, and at a meeting of St. Paul's Church Council it was decided that the following appeal should be made by the Vicar in the issue of the Church Magazine.

"Fire Watchers

'I take this opportunity of repeating my appeal for volunteers for fire-watching at the Church. At present it is only required that the person on duty on the particular night should go to the Church on hearing the siren. He or she will be provided with a key to the Vestry so that there will be free access to the Church if a fire bomb should fall on it. I hope also to have a team for each night and it will be the business of the fire-watcher to warn them if the need should arise. Volunteers please.'
N.R."

Various areas of the town were subject to enemy bombing. Abbey Road seemed to represent the flight path for the invading aircraft and streets on either side of this main road suffered terrible devastation - houses, hotels, schools, railway station, churches. Our parish was particularly affected on the nights of 3rd, 4th and 10th May. The Revd. Norman Robinson refers to these incidents in his letter of June 1941 without specifying the exact location of the homes by stating "We must give nothing away to Dr. Goebbels" - such was the extent of security at that time. How quickly we discovered that the things which are seen, our material possessions are really worthless. One night of horror and they are gone. But the unseen things, the love of God, the love of man, friendship, kindness - these things cannot be blitzed!

The column headed "In Memorium" indicates the extent of the horror of one night, 10th May, when the following residents of St. Paul's perished:-

Emily Irene Thompson Aged 40 years
Irene Mavis Thompson Aged 4 years
William Alison Hudson Aged 47 years
Mary Stobart Hudson   Aged 45 years

Richard Bold   Aged 52 years
George Wilson Carradus   Aged 40 years
Betsy Helen DrummondAged 62 years
Arthur Howard Heath   Aged 65 years
We remember these people when we listen to the names of those who died during the war at our Remembrance Day Service.

In the September 1941 issue of the Church magazine, Miss G. Fallows, Headmistress, wrote the following about damage to St. Paul's School and its consequences.

FROM OUR CHURCH SCHOOL - MAY, 1941 ....

"During the air raids of 3rd and 4th May our school building suffered structural damage, and was unfit for use until repairs had been executed.

On re-opening, ninety scholars met in the Church, where lessons were carried on for a fortnight until the Vicar (the Revd. Norman Robinson) found more suitable accommodation in the Furness Cricket Pavilion. Here the school remained for a month. Then, thanks to the expeditious efforts of the Vicar and Mr. Waddington, the school roof was mended, glass inserted in the window frames, and the caretaker, with additional help, cleared away the debris. Once again we moved, but this time with light hearts, as we returned to our true 'home'.

At 9.30 a.m. on the day of return we held a Thanksgiving Service, when appropriate hymns were sung, and Thanksgiving Prayers composed by the children were said.
MISS G. FALLOWSTWO THANKSGIVING PRAYERS

1.   O Lord our Heavenly Father, Almighty and Everlasting God, who hast safely brought us back to the school which we love, grant us safety through the coming days, that we may carry on in our school life and do our work calmly through these terrible times. For Jesus Christ's sake, AMEN.
(Howard Taylor, aged 10).

2.   Almighty Father, we offer to Thee this our simple prayer of praise and thanksgiving, for all that Thou has done for us during the past dangers. May it please Thee to guard and protect us throughout this time of war and tumult. For Jesus Christ's sake. AMEN.
(Audrey Parker, aged 10).

Audrey Parker, now Patchett, shares some of her memories of the Barrow Blitz as concerned our parish....

"I recall a sombre atmosphere and a solemn voice on the wireless (as radios were then called) announcing the outbreak of World War II. My Mother wept quietly and was comforted by my Father. So I cried too and was cuddled and comforted. I was eight years old. Clearly "War" was an awesome and terrible 'Something That Was About To Happen'.

But for a time nothing very terrible happened at all. Indeed, when my dentist was called up into the Navy, it even seemed, to an eight year old, that War was perhaps not wholly bad!

GAS ATTACKS!

There was much talk of possible air-raid gas attacks. Gas masks were issued to everyone. The domed tops of all pillar-boxes were painted with a special white paint which it was said, would change colour to indicate the presence of mustard gas. (Fortunately, the paint gradually weathered and flaked-off without ever needing to give any such dire warning). Our closest, dearest family friends - the Thompsons, who lived in Hill Road, decided to use the drawing-room, at the front of their house, as a refuge in the event of such air-raids. So they had the room made gas proof; the fire-place and all the windows were sealed and a double-doorway installed.

AIR-RAID SHELTERS.......

However, as time passed it became clear that high explosive bombing was more likely than gas attacks, so air-raid shelters with thick walls of brick, roofed with a solid slab of reinforced concrete, began to be built. Ours was built in the garden, detached from the house, but against the wall of the garage. The Thompsons had a similar shelter built in their rear garden.

MAY 1941 .....

I remember vividly the Blitz on Barrow in May of 1941. A large aircraft carrier - the Illustrious or the Indomitable - was in dock. Clearly this important ship was the objective. But much of the bombing struck residential districts of the town. An immense armour-piercing bomb hit Hawcoat Lane just some yards away from St. Paul's School. With all the neighbourhood our house, just across the road from the school, suffered considerable damage: huge holes in the roof where debris, even kerbstones, had crashed through; every window shattered; curtains in tattered shreds, ceilings collapsed; room contents dramatically re-arranged by the force of the blast; the floors inches deep in broken glass and plaster. We were thankful beyond measure, for our safety and the protection of our air-raid shelter.

Sadly, it was very different for the Thompson family. A bomb exploded in the garden at the rear of their house, their brick and concrete shelter was completely demolished. "Em" Thompson and her younger daughter, 4 year old Irene were killed. "Jim" Thompson and their older daughter, Margaret, were injured. They lay for many hours buried in rubble, before being found by rescuers and dug out. Almost the whole of their house was very severely damaged. The only part intact and unscathed was the gas-proof drawing room.

Audrey Patchett (nee Parker)

And from her Father..........

At that time (1941) St. Paul's vicarage was a large detached stone-built house in Abbey Road, just a little further along from the church. The Vicar was the Revd. Norman Robinson.

The church building lacked a Vicar's Vestry and (as a practising professional architect) I had already prepared the necessary plans for the required Vestry. The plans had been approved, but, as it was war-time, the Parochial Church Council had deemed it advisable to defer the actual building work until a more appropriate date. But, Man's plan was nullified.

A DIRECT HIT

The German bombers flew over, leaving their ghastly trade-mark: the Vicarage received a 'direct hit' and was reduced to a heap of rubble. Poor Norman had to urgently seek alternative accommodation. The heap of rubble that once sadly was St. Paul's Vicarage, was tidied up and the sand stone walling (similar to that of which the church itself was built) was carefully salvaged: with similar sandstone free and virtually on hand, our inner thoughts were running in harness with revived hopes not unconnected with that proposed vestry!

And we were, providentially, most fortunate. Living in one of those large semi-detached houses in Abbey Road, right opposite the church, was one Mr. Hugh Rainey, Barrow's leading builder with whom I had had numerous contracts on building work. Hugh Rainey became aware of the Vestry project, so I showed him a copy of the plans and we fully discussed the scheme.

A NEW VESTRY!

After due consideration, Mr. Rainey informed me that, provided he was permitted to make a selection from the stone still lying on the bombed Vicarage site, he would - as a goodwill gesture to St. Paul's - build and completely equip the proposed Vestry, all for the (ridiculous) inclusive price of £1,000! (Mr. Rainey was himself a prominent Roman Catholic).

I considered it an incredibly generous offer, the Vicar and the P.C.C. whole-heartedly agreed, and St. Paul's got its Vicar's Vestry many years earlier (and substantially cheaper) than was ever anticipated!

F.J. Parker

HAWCOAT BLITZ

The following is taken from a letter received from Peggy Hartley (nee Hayes), who was a teacher at St. Paul's School at the time of the Barrow Blitz.

"I lived in Wheatclose Road across from the school. On the first night of the bombing there was a landmine in Hawcoat Lane, and one also at the back of Armadale (i.e. the waste land next to the Rectory). The following day was spent attempting to clear up the damage - we all worked all day, but had some reservations about the Sunday afternoon strollers from undamaged areas passing by - out to see the sights"!

Mrs. Hartley goes on to tell of having to live away from Barrow for some months; and then being redeployed to St. James' School due to reduced numbers of children at St. Paul's School until they returned to their own premises. The first day back in their own building, about a month later, the blackboard still showed the date as 2nd May. It seems that not many of the pupils' fathers were in the Services, most of them being in reserved occupations.

The letter continues: "I know there were casualties in the area; my husband remembers George Hemingway, who had a drapers' business in St. Vincent Street, and who died on duty as an Air Raid Warden when the Hawcoat Lane landmine exploded".

Although never mentioned by name on the radio, Forces abroad came to realise that the "North West" town referred to in the news reports must have been Barrow as letters from home stopped getting through. The figures quoted at the time were that of eighteen thousand houses in the town, eight hundred were destroyed or rendered uninhabitable, and twelve thousand were damaged - quite incredible for one week's bombing!

Peggy Hartley

Since writing this article I have been fortunate to obtain permission from Barrow museum to use Bomb Damage photographs taken by the Civil Defence Demolition Service in 1941. In addition to the scenes here, it is interesting, though tragic, to note that land mines fell on East Mount and The Armadale Hotel, Abbey Road, adjacent to St. Paul's Vicarage which was later demolished. One fell 100 yards S.S.E. of Furness Abbey Station, and one which failed to explode fell 80 yards S.W. of Manor Farm. I was one of a number of people who went to see it. High Explosive bombs fell on No. 41 Hawcoat lane and Nos. 1 and 20 Baldwin Street.

The Photograph of the destruction in Newland Street is of particular interest to me. I was on duty in the A.R.P. Control Centre which was located in old stables underneath Michaelson Road bridge and within yards of Newland Street which was almost completely destroyed. The Control Centre had to be abandoned and the next day we re-established it in the Convent School Air Raid Shelters. My wife and baby son had just moved out to Ulverston to stay with friends after frightening experiences in Risedale Maternity Home which was also evacuated to Stanley Hospital in Ulverston the next day.

J. P. Bundy.

Almost the end!

High explosive bomb on night of 9th May 1941. Newland Street, Top End